The Raw, Un. ... . Company

FIRST EDITION

Copyright © 2017 by Paul Wagner

All rights reserved. No part of this book may be
reproduced or transmitted in any form or by any means,
electronic or mechanical, including photocopying,
recording, or by an information storage and retrieval
system, except by a reviewer who may quote brief passages
in a review to be printed in a magazine or newspaper,
without permission in writing from the publisher.

ISBN: 978-1-944671-02-0
Library of Congress: March 2017

Also from Paul Wagner Publishing:

The Field Guide to Human Personalities
The Personality Cards, The Me App
Pocket Love, Pocket People
The Colorful Me Workbook

For inquiries, visit www.PaulWagner.com

Deep heartfelt thanks to these beautiful and brilliant friends, each of whom scraped these pages and gave me lengthy, thoughtful and vital feedback.

Xiaoshen Jin, PhD., Barry Wolfman, Keith Larson, Randy Nargi, Steve Bradley & Bria Schecker

Dedication

This book is dedicated to Fred Silverman, the only real business partner I've ever had.

A creative phenomenon, Fred is the only person in history to run all three major television networks (ABC, CBS, NBC), approving every TV series that you can think of for three decades. This will never happen again.

Watching Fred work, hearing him speak and working with him were nothing short of breathtaking. He is a brilliant, generous man with an impeccable work-ethic.

Mr. Silverman put up with my bullshit for years, without complaint, and he taught me more about business and creativity than anyone in my life.

God bless you, Fred.

There will never be another you.

Table of Contents

Table of Contents

Foreword

As an investor and educator, and the co-author of <u>Venture Capital for Dummies</u>, I've attended, produced and seen thousands of startup events and thousands of hopeful pitches. Most of them are a blur of people, ideas and exit strategies, but one event stands out.

That's the one that Paul Wagner created for TIE Rockies. It had pitches for sure, but it included a hilarious collection of comedic sketches, personalities and spot-on twists on a subject that many of us take too seriously, and in some ways, not seriously enough.

There are over 10K books on startups, but you won't find anything like this one. *<u>Startup Confidential</u>* is filled with helpful advice and checklists to keep you on-track towards launching and growing a startup business.

Paul's book also provides something other startup books don't — lots of politically incorrect humor and an honest style based on Paul's many years of startup experience.

Creativity, risk-taking and laughter are fundamental parts of being human.

There's a very human side to being a startup CEO and being part of a startup team, yet there are few human endeavors that have such a high degree of uncertainty and high cost of failure.

This book provides you with more than just planning and tools, it opens a door to the psychology of startups, and all the humor that goes along with it.

Startups are about speed. Only a few hardy souls understand this. Start fast, code fast, raise fast cash, spend it, market like hell, grow 3-4X yearly and exit early. But speed doesn't create success. It's the ability to think, research and act quickly, on several fronts and in unison, that make a startup CEO successful.

Sure, everything doesn't go right all the time, but it doesn't mean that you have to "fail fast." Take sixty minutes a day and go through this book's exercises, then spend hours talking to customers.

Starting a company may seem like an insurmountable task, but if you take it sixty minutes at a time, you'll get your Big Idea up and running in no time.

Peter Adams

Co-author, *Venture Capital for Dummies*
Executive Director, Rockies Venture Club, Inc.

"The man who moves a mountain begins by carrying away small stones." ~Confucius

Disclaimer

<u>STARTUP CONFIDENTIAL</u> is a brash and humorous look at the What, Who and How of launching your Big Idea. With detailed checklists along the way, this book keeps you informed, motivated and entertained. And since humor softens egos and opens hearts, you'll find jokes sprinkled throughout every chapter.

If you've seen any of my EMMY-award winning work, this book might surprise you. While some of my books are sweet and magical, this one is more akin to swallowing a pill the size of your nephew. Packed with meaty facts and figures, the book also digs into the human aspects and the gut-wrenching stories that make startups such profound experiences.

The writing in this rough-n-tumble tome is not for the faint of heart. With playful references to sex, drugs and other fanciful delights, it's probably best you didn't share this with your cute kids. It's not really meant for story time or Junior Achievement. Capisce?

As an educational comedian, I swear like a truck driver which, *Personality Science* suggests, denotes an individual's unrelenting honesty. I tend to flair up around political correctness, invisible friends, social contrivances, and other constructs that seek to control, oppress or manipulate a living being's authenticity into working against itself.

I wrote this book because I get it. I've been down this road a 1000 times. I've garnered more rips and wrenches to my

Achilles business tendon than what feels like any human being on planet Earth.

I've had so many challenging experiences and quasi-partners, that I'm sure it's a miracle that I found Mr. Silverman. Without having worked with Fred, I'd have little faith in business and my ability to swim with sharks.

I've met a lot of executives who pose better than the wax figures at Madame Tussauds, but I don't believe that facades help anybody. Just the opposite. I believe that phony business masks and premeditated posturing compete with our honesty and require way too much upkeep. There are far better places to invest your energy. I say, "Invest in being 100% authentic."

Get real and stay that way!

If you're starting a company, I hope that this book provides the reality-check that you need. I hope that these pages save you from unnecessary heartache and anguish.

If you find it difficult to endure honesty, crass language, anti-corporate sentiments, dark thoughts, and socially-unacceptable humor, please put the book down and pleasure yourself.

After a little snack and a warm-fuzzy nap, you'll feel a lot better about EVERYTHING. I promise. Then you can continue reading my outrageous little opus.

Enjoy the book! May it lead you to happiness and profit!

Paul Wagner, Boulder, CO

March 29, 2017

Introduction

Congratulations on taking such a bold step!

You either stayed up late drinking or you spent the day on your knees praying, after which you came up with a Big Idea for your startup.

Your hypothesis elucidates the most remarkable innovation since somebody stuffed a hunk of tuna into a can. It's a miracle!

Clearly you possess an oracle's insight into the future of business and humanity. I dare say, thus begins your climb to amassing a global fortune.

While none of this is necessarily true, you might be a lover of stress and struggle, and you may not have a clue as to the perils of starting your own company, which is why you should keep reading. Although I offer jokes within these pages, startups are serious business.

Throughout the book, I'll tell you how to keep your head out of your ass, your money in your pocket, and your eyes focused on the prize.

By coming up with your Big Idea, you've put yourself in the company of powerful, disruptive entrepreneurs. Mark Zuckerberg, founder of Facebook. Steve Jobs, Apple. And Tian Wong, the inventor of the Anti-Pervert Hairy Stockings. Fascinating guy.

When starting your own company, you'll expend every ounce of energy, including reserves, you'll invest every dime of your savings, and you'll marginalize every relationship in your tree, from childhood best friends, to that hooker in Vegas, to the family members who, for some reason, still love you.

Since family members will be your first investors, keep it warm, make nice and continue to love them. Consider this an investment in your future. Luckily, we're all born into families for the same glorious reasons: To fight for limited resources and to abuse the crap out of each other. So don't get too attached.

Apparently, as a budding startup founder, you're also delusional, which is a good thing! Delusion is the only reason that anybody goes from scribbles on a napkin to quitting their day-jobs, in exchange for a 100 hr/week position, with no pay, a 92% chance of failure and a 99.6% chance of shitting the bed. Delusion can be the perverse power that keeps you going. It's fuel in the tank.

You have to love your delusion. It will protect your obsessiveness, enshrine your inner-hyperbole, keep you focused on unachievable goals, and it'll give you the confidence that you'll need to get up in front of hundreds of investors and bold-face lie to them.

I'm not advocating lying. I say this because I've heard a thousand pitches in which entrepreneurs tell stories rather than present facts. If you're honest about your business model, you'll stand out like a rock star, or well, a bunion.

Delusion will eventually be the culprit that empties your bank account, sends your mail-order bride back to Indonesia, and gives you and those you love enough reason to lose faith in humanity. But for now, consider Delusion to be your best friend, with benefits.

With all the intense and helpful information within these pages, you'll get the feeling that it's impossible to launch a successful or sustainable company. It is. This is true. It's fucking impossible.

While this book provides powerful tools, I recommend that you find something else to do with your life. Get a hobby, or even a real job like the rest of the lemmings in the world. Is Daddy flush enough to give you a fake title and paycheck?

My recommendation? Keep your day-job while you put this startup fantasy into action. Otherwise, you could lose touch with reality, relationships and your will to live. Without money, you eat less, shower less and you begin to hallucinate like a crazy person. Stinky, tweaked and broke are not the attributes of a stable, investible CEO, but you might qualify for food stamps.

By the way, I've slept in my car and once did my laundry in a FedEx-Kinko's bathroom. It wasn't pretty. Stay employed when ramping up. It'll keep you fed, clothed, sane and better able to preserve the relationships that will eventually save your life.

The key to your success is to never let anybody know how fucked up you are. You know, like when you're dating somebody new. For now, it'll be our secret that you're nuts. Double pinky swear.

I get it. You don't believe that you'll need a day-job. Regardless, this relinquishes me from any liability when you eventually fail, get depressed and impale yourself on a lawn dart.

Who am I? I am a serial entrepreneur, a startup addict, an EMMY® award winning comedian, a corporate educator, and someone who's made every known startup mistake. I've also had my ass handed to me ten times over, in five different languages.

By reading this book, you put yourself on the path to building a multinational conglomerate, launching your own planet, and having your footprints bronzed and put on display at Walgreens - NATIONWIDE. You're gonna make trillions!

This is the moment I tell you good luck, enjoy the book and hire me to speak at your next event.

Seriously, hire me to speak. I'm hilarious.

What Is a Startup?

A startup is a new company, usually less than three years old. It can have anywhere from $500 personal cash to $1.5MM of venture capital in the bank.

Startups are unforgiving beasts. They'll eat you alive if you let them, but they can also fund your retirement and yield you enough cash to buy three houses.

Most startups have one to four founders, two to ten employees, three advisors, three investors, one exhausted, sexually harassed intern, a keg on tap, and a little blue jar in the back of the fridge stuffed with two ounces of sticky-icky. Ya know, pot.

In many cases, your first investors will be family members or other folks who respond enthusiastically to guilt. If you do not know what guilt is, just ask your Jewish and Catholic friends. We all grew up on chicken soup, Wheaties, and the kind of guilt that would make your skin crawl.

Startups are also hotbeds for hilarity, chaos and miscommunication. You'll make friends, lose friends, lose money and eventually find yourself working at Costco, in a good way. Up until the final decree of your divorce and seconds before your nervous breakdown, it'll be a great ride, roughly ten minutes.

Startup founders should be prepared for roller coaster rides, chock-full of swinging-door relationships, epic life lessons and excruciating, demoralizing ass-kickings.

You'll drink a lot of local craft beers, meet a ton of people, find out how fucked-up you are, and learn that you're in good company. You might even get laid.

Startups usually begin with $20,000 "First Money" from Mom, Dad, best friend Timmy or stranger Bob. After First Money, the company's founders will continue to sink their own cash into the venture, which they'll do until long-after they're bankrupt and living at the Y. This is because most founders are too embarrassed to admit that their company failed just ten minutes after you gave them your life savings.

Startup founders will spend more money on their own businesses than on their weddings and well-being, which is why so many founders are pale.

If you have a girlfriend or boyfriend, husband or wife, life-partner or imaginary sex slave, you're going to want to convince them that co-funding your venture is the best way to prove how much they love you.

Promise them nothing, but be REALLY nice so that they continue to fund your wobbly boat. Some say this is manipulation, but it's only manipulation if you're not sincere. Are you sincere? Of course you are!

Some founders tell such whopping lies that everybody begins to think that they're God-children or alien beings from a distant galaxy. This might attract venture capital firms for a millisecond, but you'd better be prepared before meeting with them. If you don't have a buttoned-up presentation that's backed by research, you'll come off like a circus clown.

You might also try to fund your startup through revenue. What is revenue? It's when your company actually charges money for its product. Crazy, right?

I know that this is unheard of in today's startup scene, but history shows that somebody at some point charged customers for the privilege of taking home their products. You can quote me on that.

Most startup founders are so filled with their own essence, that they think that they're going to be on CNN before the end of the week, when the truth is, they'll barely make it out of their moms' basements. It takes a mature person to balance enthusiasm with preparedness.

While anybody can start a company, it will take dedicated founders, stable and sober, each with expertise in the company's market category, to build a ship that's sustainable and relevant. Cute marketing hooks, free beer and hipster t-shirts only go so far.

To best founders avoid the traps of believing their own bullshit. A surefire way to keep yourself in check is to land quality mentors and advisors. They'll help you live in a grounded reality rather than in the contrived startup theme park that you've built in your head.

When founders are out-of-whack, they'll even hire secretaries to take notes at meetings that they have with THEMSELVES! This is delusion in the highest degree.

Be passionate about your startup. Your relentless passion can be the deciding ingredient that tips investors in your favor. Imagine a dispassionate car salesman, a passive prostitute, or an unassertive football player. Silly, right? Nut up and get excited or go get fitted for a monogramed barista outfit. Be deeply motivated and go for the gold.

Responsible startup founders are careful. They don't become addicted to tweets from their stoned friends that say, "Awesome app, brah!". They continually critique their own ideas, approaches and successes. They spend prudently, scale modestly and are on a never-ending hunt for customers. They're animals!

As things heat up and your startup hits the news, you'll feel like a million bucks. Just don't let it go to your head. Stay grounded and stay the course.

There ya have it! If you're not completely flipped out, pissed-off, discouraged or overwhelmed, continue reading. You're off to a great start!

Startup CEOs spend more time seeking validation for their personalities and ideas than they do exploring the real-world potential of their products and markets.

Don't be this person. He's a bonehead.

FunFacts

Top Cities for
Startups & Entrepreneurs *

Boulder, Denver, Fort Collins & Loveland, CO
Cambridge, Newton & Framingham, MA
Seattle & Bellevue, WA
Iowa City & Ames, IA
San Fran, San Jose, Sunnyvale & Santa Clara, CA
Washington, DC
Arlington & Alexandria, VA
Cheyenne, WY
Dallas, Houston & San Antonio, TX
Chapel Hill & Charlotte, NC
Corvallis, OR
Bozeman, MT
Ann Arbor & East Lansing, MI
Madison, WI
Miami, Tampa & Orlando, FL
Rochester, MN
Manhattan, KS
Bloomington, IN
Brookings, SD
Cincinnati & Columbus, OH
Baltimore, MD
Las Vegas, NV
Atlanta, GA

(*) Fortune.com, Kauffman Foundation

2 Your Big Idea

What is a Big Idea? It's a notion that leads to the creation of a product that is believed to improve life as we know it. Obvious examples include Penicillin, Bar Codes, Lyft and the mega-God of life-savers, Pringles Potato Chips.

Before you start planning a celebratory SpaceX trip to Mars, be sure that your Big Idea hasn't already been created and sold in the market. You might be surprised to find out that somebody has already made millions selling inflatable puppies. Do the research.

Sometimes identical ideas dawn on several people at the same time. From Marconi, Edison and Tesla to Musk, Gates and your cousin Joey, it happens to the best of us. The most nimble and aggressive get the big prize.

Without a Big Idea, you don't stand a chance of launching a startup. Cute little ideas aren't worth your time, plus they make investors want to run face-first into brick walls. Inaugurate your magical mystery startup tour with a bonafide Big Idea.

Just like delusion can be your fuel, so can a hint of craziness. Craziness will make you stand out from the hipster, bro-crowd and help you attract the impossible. Just don't get arrested.

Repeat after me: "I want to build a startup company. Therefore, I am a danger to myself and others. Please approach slowly and with no sudden movements."

The average non-crazy person walks around thinking, "Today I will buy milk so that I can have it for coffee in the morning. Then I will drink it and be happy while I drive to work. Because I am normal."

The average batshit founder says, "I have to raise money for this fuckin' thing. I am awesome, but holy crap I AM STRESSED! This product is a paradigm shift! Is it okay to drink scotch before 10am? Fuck, I forgot my girlfriend's name. Am I thinking from my conscious mind or the eternal mind? Mommy, before I go out into the real world, can we cuddle one more time?"

Anyone who runs a startup business or finds themselves reading this book probably has a few issues. At least we're in this together!

Do your research so that you can stay ahead of the curve and avoid building things like apps that help men be more chauvinistic. Keep in mind that if you move too slowly, you might appear to be moving backwards. And always give your consumers more, rather than less, credit.

Dig deep into your inspiration to source the most enduring gold.

Write down your Big Idea right now. Note its ten most distinctive attributes. Outline ten of its most alluring premises and promises. Derive ten of the most remarkable off-shoots of your product.

The reason that you do all of this work is because you might find that your best, most customer-friendly product is a derivation of your original Big Idea, but three levels down.

After your initial exploration, don't fantasize for too long about derivatives. You won't have the time or money to build them. I bang my head on the table every time I hear entrepreneurs say, "Oh! And if we change the product in 15 ways brah, we'll be rich!" No doofus, by spinning in 15 different directions, you'll get dizzy, puke all over yourself and go broke.

With a well-defined Big Idea, you're ready to chisel out a stunning 30-second pitch. Your "elevator pitch" is your calling card. It should be an inspiring, easy-to-understand statement that outlines what your product is, who needs it and why, all in under 30 seconds. Be eager to rattle this off on a moment's notice and with a passion that embodies a slightly manic insanity.

To learn if your Big Idea has real-world value, speak to potential customers and ask them about their pain points. A pain point is something in their business lives that could be made easier. Working, for example.

To be successful, your product will have to soothe real pains of actual human beings, unlike Edible Gloves, Diet Water, Squirrel Underpants and The Inflatable Unicorn Horn for Cats.

I cringe when I hear founders say, "My product doesn't need customers brah, it just needs eyeballs." If you hear a newbie CEO say this, excuse yourself to the bathroom and climb out the window.

As a founder, your job is to deliver a solid product to the marketplace and sell as many as you can. Impress 1000 customers to the point where they can't stop fantasizing about you in their bathtub. Start small, innovate quickly and continue to enroll paying fanatics.

Wait, are you trying to tell me that to be successful, I'll need real customers? Yes, Einstein. This is how your company will make money, ya know, from people paying for your products. You'll learn how to interview potential customers so that they provide you with insanely valuable intel, in the next chapter entitled, "Customer Discovery".

Without revenue, your next three years will be filled with fast food, heartburn and couch-surfing. Remember: Couch-surfing gets old after two nights, unless you're having sex with the host. In that case, three.

Congratulations on having a Big Idea! You are now one step closer to owning a 25-room mega-yacht, commanding your new Apache Attack Helicopter, sporting the world's first glow-in-the-dark ass implants and owning Platinum Cabin tickets on the world's first one-way mission to Mars. The world awaits your genius!

Honor your Big Idea by exploring its value for specific sets of customers. Research concepts that are similar to yours, so that you're able to defend your Big Idea's unique merits, benefits, attributes and worth.

3 Customer Discovery

If you can't rattle off at least three real-world, customer pain points, you don't know your customers and you might not have a viable product. We'll get you there!

How do you get to know your customers' pains? You need an understanding of The Socratic Method. Oh and you'll need a list of potential customers. You have to speak with real human beings. You can't just make this shit up, right?!

What the heck is The Socratic Method? It's the process of asking questions that draw out beliefs and assumptions, in pursuit of the purest, most potent answers.

Using this method will help you hone your products into valuable solutions that heal the pains of your customers. With real solutions, customers will be more inspired to pay for your product. This is how you'll make money.

With your customer list in hand, make phone calls and set meetings. Don't pitch products or try to sell anything. Just ask everybody what makes their jobs harder than they should be. They're itchin' to tell somebody! Be a gentle observer. Be the priest, but not the one that molests kids.

Ask your average startup monkeys if they've spoken with customers and they'll say, "Why would I do that, brah?!

That would ruin it! My ex-girlfriend's roommate and her dealer love our stuff!"

Don't indulge in validation coming from friends, family and sex partners. That's like heroin to you and your business. Get off the needle and talk to customers.

Here are the questions NOT to ask your customers:

1. If we built a product that did A and B, would you pay $100 per month for 12 years? Plus a deposit?

2. Look at our awesome prototype! Isn't it disruptive!? Do you wanna buy it right now or do you wanna wait until the blue ones come out?

3. Can I give you our cool product when we're done so that you can tell us how awesome it is? I'll give you a gift card for every five-star review you post!

Here's an example of a Socratic customer discovery:

1. What are the most painful processes and procedures that you come across in your job?

2. How much time do you spend on these painful processes? Are there other unmet needs?

3. Are you addressing any of these pain points?

4. Tell me about other company-wide pain points. How are you involved in the related processes?

5. What do you think would help resolve or improve these conditions?

At follow-up meetings, explore the attributes of your products. Ask questions that explore your hypotheses, but do not lead with these questions in the first meeting.

Subsequent meetings will help you turn acquaintances into customers, at which point you'll ask questions that lead to validating your products and your customer segments. Take it slow and follow up upon key updates.

Coming out of the gate firing off product-pointed questions is like a poker player shooting his mouth off before seeing his opponent's four aces. Don't be intoxicated with your own ambition and ideas.

Too many startups build prototypes then jump into hiring sales people, refusing to do any customer interviews to prove their assumptions. I just want to smack these people in the heads — then invoice them for my time.

Stay humble. Once in the Socratic groove, the results will blow you away.

We all dream of creating super-successful startups, imaging ourselves to be the Chosen Ones, awakened by the most enlightened, anointed ideas. But even religions sell products born from real-world pain. Whether it's forgiveness or everlasting life, they're selling products that drive (attract) revenue.

Whether it's ideologies or gadgets, money flows when people need them. Less need means less sales. Less sales, less revenue. Less revenue, no salary. With no salary, you're back on the pole or looking for a job.

"But wait brah! What about products that come to us in our dreams or when we're posing with our hipster buds? Just because we don't do customer whatever, doesn't mean that they're not valuable, right?"

Fair question. Of course they're valuable. Every tiny thought you have is valuable. They're just not valuable to anybody but you.

The more that you empathize with real customer pains, the more you'll uncover compelling value propositions (what's in it for your customers at your price point). That's how to drive toward success.

After you engage in **NO LESS THAN 100** customer interviews, pick one of the pain points (problems) that you learned about and develop a product for it, or pivot your product into a solution that solves one of the problems you uncovered. Makes sense, right?

Seek to solve real problems rather than tripping on the fake ones that you invented while high on chocolate-covered espresso beans.

Get real. If you've got a product that doesn't solve problems, then you don't have an investment-worthy business. You might have a lawn ornament or holiday trinket that you can sell at church functions, but venture capital will elude you.

Examples of Problems & Solutions

Problem #1: In the early 1900s, many people worked 30 miles from their homes. They needed regular, daily, individualized transportation.

Solution #1: In the 1900s, automobiles were perfected. They could fit more than one person and functioned well on dusty, undeveloped roadways.

Problem #2: In the early 1400s, European books were mostly hand-written. It would take months to copy just one book by hand (although the Chinese figured out printing presses in 1040AD).

Solution #2: Gutenberg's printing press improved on Western machines. By 1600, his presses created over 200 million books. It changed life as we knew it.

Problem #3: When a person picks their nose and eats it, he ingests bacteria that can make him sick as hell.

Solution #3: Winston Oliver Marsh invented a pinky-condom for safe booger collection, and a patent-pending hypoallergenic booger rinse, allowing the picker to eat cleaner, healthier, nutritious boogers.

Your product, based on your Big Idea, should be a big solution to big problems. When building your investor presentations, one of your first slides will be "The Problem." Your next slide will be "The Solution." This is why this chapter is so important.

Once you engage potential customers in Socratic-style dialogues, you'll be well on your way to raising a billion dollars, owning a flying car and celebrating your first of several attention-grabbing heart attacks. What could be more fun?! How about IBS?! Yes please!

If your Big Idea isn't wildly disruptive, it must solve specific pain points of large sets of customers. Otherwise, you'll waste a lot of people's time, including your own.

Finding Your Why

To do anything in the startup world, you've got to know Why you're doing it. It has to come from a personal place, deep within your spiritual core.

If you don't have a spiritual core, you might be a robot, which means that you're exponentially more employable than the rest of the world. Kudos!

If your Why is to be rich enough to own three Teslas, it's not compelling enough to drive the growth of a startup. That's the kind of goal you'd hear from stoned teenagers. If money is your primary Why, you'll never work smart enough to lead the company to success. Remember, you'll be broke for a few years, so making money can't be a key motivator. Be thoughtful when choosing a Why.

While there's a certain cachet to running a startup, especially a funded one, you must be in it for the long haul. Without a long-tail Why, you might give up long before your designers finish your first logo.

Here are a few examples of Whys that I find inspiring:

1. My mother died of cancer and I longed to help her in her final months. We later learned that chemotherapy was more toxic for her than the alternative methods

we explored. I'm committed to helping others learn about and embrace alternative, non-chemical therapies for advanced stages of cancer and other painful diseases.

2. I fell in love with sports at 10 yrs old, when a famous baseball player asked me to be his batboy. I've always wanted to make him proud. This is why I'm so committed to this sports app. It speaks to the little boy in me.

3. I believe medical information should be understandable and accessible by everyone. As a nurse, I've seen hundreds of people become confused when reading medical pamphlets. I'm committed to developing technologies that improve a patient's comprehension, so that they can better understand their conditions and prognosis.

Aren't these beautiful? Can't you just feel the universe sitting up straight and coming to the rescue? These are the types of Whys that hit home runs.

I meet countless entrepreneurs who have Whys that sound like they came out of a book entitled, "Things I Say When I'm High." Here are a few quotes that I've heard founders say at actual startup events:

1. I'm really good at making this shit, man! So I figure, why not? Somebody's gotta do it!

2. I built one and it kinda worked, so we're gonna start a company and see how it goes.

3. There's no way I'm working for some butthole, so I might as well do this instead.

You'll work yourself to the bone for at least three years. What's the motivation? Is your heart really involved in this or do you just like being a quotable, player on the startup red carpet?

Don't let your desire to be a startup hipster distract you from being sincere. If a Why isn't coming to mind, meditate on it. Allow a deep, honest and relevant Why to surface. Wait on it. Wait on a Why that's real. Wait, wait, wait. Or hook up with another startup founder who's already living from a compelling Why. Don't rush to leave your day-job or employment situation until you arrive at a Why that inspires you to your core.

When you can verbalize and embody a captivating Why, you might have enough of the right stuff to drive your startup toward success.

If your Why doesn't inspire and motivate you, something or someone else could easily steal your attention, leaving your startup and its investors in the dust.

FunFacts

According to the Global Entrepreneurship Monitor (GEM), there are over 27 million entrepreneurs in the United States. *

95% of entrepreneurs hold a bachelor's degree or higher. *

Human birth control pills work on gorillas. *

92% of all startups fail. The rest of them don't necessarily do very well. *

93% of people who accept counter-offers will leave within 18 months. This means that compromise is not always beneficial. *

(*) Inc Magazine, Forbes, Wall Street Journal, Fast Company, Startup Bros GemConsortium.org, Bootstrike.com

5 First Money

It's exciting when you first realize that your Big Idea might be valuable enough to attract funding. You can almost taste its future! With each passing moment, you feel increasingly invincible!

The problem is: Where do you find the money to get your life-changing product out into the world? Seriously, without mass-adoption, how are you going to buy that island? You have to source the cash!

With thousands of investors throughout the world and millions of ideas in play, you have to ask yourself, "How am I going to entice a big risk-taker to fork over his savings and fund my brilliant, one-page plan?" Well, guess what! You already know your first investor.

It's YOU!

While family, friends and sweethearts will be the real "First Money" to fill the coffers of your dream, you are most likely your first investor. Congratulations!

Keep in mind that your $500 to $2500 investment isn't enough to be considered "First Money," but you're now an investor in AND the CEO of a slightly, partially, if you squint, funded startup! GOOSE BUMPS!

Thank heavens you have some cash to burn, because you're going to need it to build a proof of concept, which is your company's first product in its most rudimentary form. This is also referred to as a working prototype or MVP (minimum viable product), whereby early adopters of your product can enjoy enough features to give them confidence and make them fans.

Do you have the money or skills to build an MVP? If so, awesome! If it's strong enough, it'll be easier to entice your first customers to pay for the privilege of owning your glow in the dark, velcro doohicky. With paying customers, investors will love you.

When a startup gains momentum via revenue or fans, a captivating CEO can inspire family, friends and sweethearts to put some real money into their Big Idea. THIS is called "First Money." Depending on your market and what you're selling, your First Money could be anywhere from $20K to $150K. It all depends on the costs of proving your concept or plan.

Getting First Money feels kinda like when the cool kid in high school sat next to you at lunch. Even if he did it by accident, you got immediate validation and your stock went up. It's the same with startups.

First Money is different than Seed Capital because it usually comes from people you know. Seed usually comes from serious or accredited investors. More on that later in the Joys of Raising Money chapter.

After raising First Money, it's exponentially easier to attract other investors to fund the building of your Apple-Face-Twit.org, so that you can become the ruler of the known universe.

If you already have First Money, or better yet, angel or seed investment, way to go! Your presentation must be flawless, or it's filled with more baloney than an Oscar Mayer piñata. Regardless, you're on your way!

As much as you think you'll be at $100MM revenue in three weeks, which only proves how unstable you are, you'll be raising money for the life of your startup. You will ALWAYS be raising money, even when you're in the bathroom.

You'll think about raising money, and you'll make plans around raising money, 24 hours a day. Soon enough, you'll easily prefer tattooing your labia or popping the zits on your balls to raising capital. It fucking sucks.

You will perpetually be raising money because startups are evil, selfish, cavernous, eternal black holes born from the darkness in the universe. While they seem like a sure thing, they're nothing but a question that may or may not have an answer.

If you know that you have something special in your Big Idea and if you've found a few potential customers who'll love your product upon building it, you've got to find a way to build the first version of your product.

Having money in the bank can be dangerous for some founders. Since they've never spent investment money before, they have no way of knowing what's important and what's superfluous. They'll use the money to rent offices, install hot tubs and buy fancy t-shirts. Please don't do this, because it would mean you're an idiot.

Here's what you do with First Money:

1. Find three brilliant advisors in your business category, who also love what you're doing. Ask them to help you form the foundational ideas and operating procedures for your company.

2. Research what it will cost to build a working, sellable version of your product. Before building it, ask a few potential customers if it's the kind of product that solves their real-world pain points.

3. If the advisors and customers think it's a good idea to build your product the way you've envisioned it, then go for it.

4. If you don't have unanimous support, slow down and continue your research. Save your First Money for building your MVP. Only spend it when it's absolutely necessary and the right time.

With a great idea and a little cash, you're a danger to yourself and your startup. Seek advice from seasoned advisors about running tight operations with trim budgets. Most startups go broke in three months.

6 Inc. Like a Boss

Many startup founders jump the gun. They come up with a Big Idea and 20 minutes later they're steeped in volumes of legalese, forming a bonafide C-corp. While this shows initiative, it's crazy overkill.

If you want to start a company, make sure you have a product or service to sell first. If the endeavor involves other people, you'll want to incorporate with a structure that protects you and your partners, especially if one of your friends is clueless or litigious. Litigious is a French word meaning Asshole.

Incorporating costs less money than dinner for two at Chipotle. It's fairly simple in the US and UK, and it doesn't take much paperwork to keep it up to date.

While I'm not a lawyer and nothing in this book is legal advice, everything you'll need to start your company is probably found on government websites. There are LLCs, S-corps, C-corps, B-corps and more, all of which have unique structures, levers and protections.

The most simple corporate structure is an LLC, which easily converts to more complex structures (S-corp or C-corp) when things heat up. By heating up, I mean an investor bought into your bullshit and wrote a check.

Here are the primary company structures:

LLC

A Limited Liability Company has members who can't be held personally liable for company debts. Hybrid entities, they combine the characteristics of a corporation with a partnership or sole proprietorship. With LLCs, you don't have to submit annual paperwork and get migraines. Although it's not the right structure for when you have stock holders, an LLC will quickly make you legit.

S-Corp

A Subchapter S (S Corporation) meets specific IRS requirements and is the way to go if you're a small company that has friends and family as investors. With 100 shareholders or less, you'll have the benefit of incorporation while being taxed as a partnership. It's the cuter version of a C-corp.

C-Corp

The "C" in C-corp stands for cocaine. As in, you'll need some if you want to get through all the paperwork before your next birthday. This structure is for serious companies with serious investors. It's taxed separately from its owners and has all the bells and whistles to make your shareholders happy.

501 (c)

A 501(c) is a nonprofit organization that doesn't pay taxes, even if it's a religion that does nothing but buy robes and maintain expensive real estate. To be a 501(c), you have to fall under one of these purposes: charitable, religious, educational, scientific, literary, public safety testing, amateur sports competitions, or preventing cruelty to children or animals.

B-Corp

The "B" stands for benefit. This is a hybrid that mixes the juicy greed of a C-corp with the good-will in a 501(c). You can show gobs of profit, buy islands and help others at the same time. Woohooo! This structure has the stock attributes of a C-corp and the tax benefits of a non-profit. It's great for positive impact-missions that seek to benefit society, workers, communities, the environment and your bank account.

Sole Proprietorship

This is not a corporate entity. It's a fancy term that means you and your business are married. It refers to the person who owns the business, who is the same person responsible for its debts.

There ya have it, the main structures to consider for your company. Choose wisely and keep it simple for as long as you can. Start with an LLC and convert into an S-corp or C-corp when investors arrive.

Do not overcomplicate your life with 300 pages of incorporation and operating agreements. There's plenty of time for this after your first $100K of capital or revenue. Plus, who has time for 300 pages? I can barely get through a children's picture book.

A while back, I was working with a brilliant, seasoned business person who required that we have a 200 page business plan, a complex corporate structure, a 50 page operating agreement, five accountants, four lawyers, six employees, two Keurigs, a Lichtenstein and a butler. This was all before we had a product.

What I love about this experience is that working with this man was 10x more valuable than getting an MBA. What I didn't so much love is that they required such complexity in our paperwork that I was only able to have erections every other holiday.

Complexity in your startups puts a great deal of stress on your partnerships. It can also negatively impact the development of a product and customer base. In simple terms, complexity means you're always moments away from a massive myocardial infarction (heart attack). If you'd like to avoid this, keep your legal and operating paperwork down to a dull roar.

If you're writing what feels like an international best-selling novel to memorialize the agreement between you and the other founders, you're asking for more stress and trouble than is necessary.

In exchange for the most complex incorporation and operating documents, most startup lawyers will put you on payment plans that eventually add up to the salary of a full-time executive. It's a waste of money and lawyers aren't here to help, they're con artists.

While certainly convincing, lawyers are not working on your behalf. They are looking to hook you and other passionate, unsuspecting fools into a game I like to call,

"Let Me Bill You For Every Fucking Breath." This is an exciting game whereby instead of owning a car, you take the bus and pay your lawyer until you're 70.

If you feel that you truly need a lawyer's services for incorporating, find one that you like and start by asking for their advice. Don't contract them or pay them anything. Just get their two cents and see if you can glean enough information so can do it yourself. Check out the Legal Bullshit chapter later in the book.

Be gentle with yourself when incorporating. Keep it simple, trust your founding partners, and let the process of incorporation unfold naturally.

If it ain't nobody but you, don't incorporate until you have a product you love. You can still file patents and trademarks, but if you're alone on this thing, incorporating is probably not yet necessary.

If you spend more time incorporating and writing agreements than creating products and building customer relationships, you're masturbating. Stop it. You'll go blind.

Co-Working Spaces

With their stocked kitchens and designer furniture, you'll always feel fresh, new and relevant at your local co-working space. Some people thrive in these environments, while others feel that they're way too packed with uppity socializers and expensive snacks.

These friendly havens can be found in just about every major city in the US, Europe and beyond. While to some they are the ultimate workplace, to others they are social playgrounds with free smoothies and expensive in-house convenience stores.

While co-working has become the rage, it also has a few limitations. Keep the following things in mind as you evaluate where you might be most productive.

1. With open spaces the size of football fields, co-working offices are built in ways that inspire people to avoid work altogether. Members are so relaxed, they drink beer at 10am, walk around in their underwear and enjoy farting on command.

2. Too many white people! That's because non-caucasians are way too educated to pay for expensive hippie lounges full of chatty, shallow crackers.

3. All the hipster clothes and artfully trimmed beards might cause you to feel fashion-challenged.

4. Co-working spaces often have crazy expensive classes, while the same classes can be found online for free.

5. There is so much chatter and product evangelizing in these places that it's difficult to think clearly.

6. These open offices are like zoos, except they're filled with animals who aren't quite as intelligent as say, monkeys, tigers and bears.

To be fair, co-working offices are excellent, affordable alternatives to longer-term office leases. For the individual or two to three person teams, they're perfect.

Most co-working places also offer private offices, but do you really need privacy? Are personal ping-pong tables and couches a must? I doubt you need either of these things when spending other people's money.

In addition to coffees and teas, these beautiful spaces have beer, Kombucha and hills of freshly ground espresso, the latter of which will keep you brainstorming for years. Some might say that brainstorming is much easier than developing a real product. Hmmmm.

Consider striking a deal with your favorite co-working space by choosing a limited plan, for example, 20 hours per week. The other 20 hours you can continue to lounge around naked and fuck off at home, like you usually do.

Socialize often, but focus on product development that stems from customer discovery. Co-working can be distracting.

Checklist #1

Bang out in under an hour:

- [ ] Expand on your Big Idea by writing out your founding vision and potential derivatives.

- [ ] Write a 30-second description of your Big Idea and the related company (your elevator pitch).

- [ ] Explore and arrive at a compelling Why.

- [ ] Write a list of your founders.

- [ ] Write a list of the people that you would like to eventually have as your key team members.

- [ ] Write a list of potential customers to interview for your Customer Discovery.

- [ ] If you landed First Money, send a Thank You note and thoughtful gift to your new investors.

Requires additional time and effort:

- [ ] Register an LLC or Limited Partnership with your city, state, region or province.

- [ ] Research and contract an inexpensive office or a co-working space.

- [ ] Establish a schedule that allows you to have time for your loved ones and your hobbies.

- [ ] Select a book from the Author's Favorites (at the end of this book). Finish reading it within a week.

- [ ] Regularly exercise or go for long brisk walks.

- [ ] Do something insanely fun or adventurous today.

Product Prep

Some startup founders become so excited, that they forget to develop their product, treating it like a 3rd cousin. What's the point of 3rd cousins, anyway?

These founders might raise money and build a prototype, but they often have no idea how to use it, sell it, improve it or deliver it. This is because some startup CEOs are product-driven, while others are business-driven. You might be one, both or neither.

To prepare your product so that you can either enter the market or raise money, you will need to dig deep into your product's identity and development, as if your future depends on it. Because it does.

Throw away the tainted validation you've internalized and all the warm-fuzzy kudos that came from your brother, grandmother, extended family, and the cute cashier at the mall. It's all useless.

Product owner (or product manager) is the title of the person who can take your product from *meh* to WOASH! If you're not a product owner rock star, you'd better find one.

Product owners/managers know how to adapt products according to the learning that occurs during customer discovery. You need a product rock star right now! These elusive geniuses are hard to find, but they'll save your reputation and your ass.

I once purchased a product from a rising star startup during their flashy hipster launch. Instead of readying the product for real customers, it was clear to me that their product owner had spent six months blowing himself. There were more mindless shiny people stroking each other's vacuousness at that launch party than I've seen at any political convention or cult. When I tested the product, it didn't work, so I immediately complained. The CEO told me that I should be more compliant since I'm in the startup biz and that I should spend a few hours with him so he can improve his product.

I said, "No you presumptuous nitwit, you don't tell strangers to give you half of their day in exchange for the anti-privilege of suffering the pains of speaking with you. Do your homework before you ship. Nurture a real relationship before asking someone to cup your balls. Get off your egoistic pedestal. Now compensate me for wasting my time. I want a 3X refund."

Answering the following questions will not only help you nail down your product and establish an integrity-based process, your answers will help you populate your investor presentation, and create a more stable foundation for your company's future.

If you skip these questions, you'll struggle to create the right slides for your presentation, which should showcase your startup in the most magnificent light.

Some say, "Jump off the cliff and grow wings on the way down!" The people who say this either have serious attention-deficit issues, they refuse to be prepared, or they're lying in a riverbed right now with broken bones looking up at a cliff.

Given all the competition for startup capital, your best bet is to focus on the quality development and delivery of your product, how it solves real problems and how it fits into the market.

Use the following list of migraine-inducing questions as your guide to explore your Big Idea and its related products. Startup founders often avoid these questions saying, "Questions are such a buzz-kill, brah!". Rather than cultivate futures based on analyses, they prefer remaining high on their ideas. Nobody said this would be a cocktail party hermano! Enjoy your research!

Product

- Do you have a serious product owner to push the delivery of something awesome?

- What are the primary value propositions of your product? In other words, what aspects of your products meet customer pain points?

- What do your products do? Why are you certain that they solve real-world problems?

- What does your product look, feel and sound like? Is your product ready for sale?

- Are you spending enough time enjoying your product and startup? If not, you better get to it!

- What is the status of product development? What is the process for advancing your product? How would you describe your phases of development?

- Do you have a prototype or MVP (minimal viable product)? How are you paying to build it?

- If it's already built, is it working properly? Did you test multiple scenarios? Did you let customers beat you up a little bit, and did you listen to them?

Market

- How will you market the your products?

- What is your brand? Do your products share the company name or are they separate brands?

- What is your market category? Which industry? Which verticals within the industry?

- When do you plan on entering the market (to sell)?

- If marketing stresses you out, please raise your hand. Thank you.

- What type of team will be required to get to market?

- Do you know how marketing is evolving and what categories of marketing are best for your brand?

- Are you reading marketing blogs and reading books?

Customers

- What segments of the population will buy your product? Can you describe each type of customer?

- Why will these customers buy? Are you sure this is the best product for them, given their problem?

- What is your test market? When does testing start?

- How did you pivot or change your product based upon the testing and learning?

Sales & Distribution

- What are the distribution channels for your product?

- How and where does it get sold? If it requires a sales team, what's your plan to build one?

Competitors

- Who are your primary competitors? How are they each unique? What makes your products unique?

Pricing & Revenue

- What does your product cost? Why this price-point?

- How did you determine the price of your product?

- How will you find your first paying customers? How will you keep them?

There's no reason to rush to answer these questions. Answer a few now and continue to return to them as you develop your presentation (see "The Presentation" chapter). Once you answer all of them, you'll be miles ahead of 99% of startups on planet Earth.

If you can't successfully defend your product to a specific group of customers, then you probably don't have a marketable product and you won't be appealing to investors.

Operating Plans & Agreements

Run your startup as if every time you waste money, it takes a year of life away from your mom or the old lady next door. This'll keep you on your toes!

To run a successful company, you need a well-constructed operating plan and clear, concise operating agreements. These do not have to be complicated, but they should be thorough.

You will never get a concise document from a lawyer without paying out the ass, so plan on writing the first version yourself or with your co-founders.

You might consider asking other startup founders for copies of their operating agreements. They can white-out private information and you can buy them a beer. That'll save you three months of a founder's salary.

Operating Plans

An operating plan is a list of actions and drivers that support the company's mission and strategies. In suburban-family lingo, your operating plan is an outline of play-dates and kitchen chores. OMG! Mom, can Craig sleep over?!

More defined, an operating plan is a list of people, titles, duties, deliverables and timelines laid out in a way that helps you, your co-founders, employees and interns understand who is in charge, who is doing what, and how the company plans on moving forward on a daily, weekly, monthly and yearly basis. This plan should drive you to revenue and beyond.

Your first operating plan doesn't have to be an award winning novel. It's a starting point. It might be messy or written with crayons on construction paper. That's okay, as long as it's thorough.

You need an operating plan to drive and keep track of all the aspects and players in your company. For example: Tom finds customers while Sally builds products, and by March we start making big sales. Then we can hire Joey.

Learn how to map out how your company will achieve success. Eventually, your plan should tie everything together and include how you are spending money (expenses) and making money (revenue).

Consider using project management tools (apps and software) to keep you and your teams organized. As this category is constantly evolving, research the latest innovators and get organized quickly.

Project tools will help you keep your head out of your ass. Even while smoking pot 24/7, if you can read, you'll be able to restate your progress to everyone involved. These tools will also help you to delegate so that you have more free time to worship yourself.

If you don't have an operating plan, then you'll have a difficult time defending how your startup makes money, especially when speaking with investors and those who have measurable intellects.

When it comes to Operating Plans: Create your plan, work your plan. Improve your plan. Work your plan.

Operating Agreements (OA)

This is a legal contract stating how founders benefit or behave upon certain events and milestones. It's vital that you and your co-founders come to terms.

Your OA should outline who has voting rights, how member/owners will govern the business and how finances will be managed. For S-corps, C-corps and B-corps, your operating agreements are called Corporate By-Laws. It's all the same thing.

For example:

1. *Sally is CEO, Tom is CMO, Joey is an asshole.*

2. *If Sally dies, her husband gets the stock. If Joey dies, we buy a keg. Tom can't die.*

3. *Interns do all the work and we can't have sex with them until maybe the Christmas party.*

4. *Sally gets paid more than everybody else because her brain is 3x bigger than everybody's combined.*

5. *Joey has to clean the bathrooms.*

6. *Transgenders are safe and cool, always.*

7. *If Sally gets pregnant, she doesn't have to come to work until her kid is 12, but she still gets paid.*

8. *Tom's not that bright so we'll pay for his training.*

9. *If anybody punches the dog, they're fired.*

10. *If two of the founders don't like the third founder, the third founder must be a fuck-tard. He will have to resign, unless he gives us cash and donuts.*

In their OAs, startups often forget to state under which circumstances a founder can be removed as an employee. The biggest challenges in startups are the conflicts between co-founders. Outline all the reasons and processes required for canning a founder.

When bringing on new people and investors, make sure the co-founders retain voting majority for as long as possible. This will help you protect your creation from disruptive buttheads.

When you hire people, include a non-compete clause in their contracts. This states that they cannot work for a competing company or promote a competing product while working for you. It's reasonable to make the term of a non-compete one to two years.

What isn't reasonable is making everybody from the pizza boy to the janitor sign away their freedom away with a non-compete just because you're under the illusion that you figured out why Frankenstein failed. Whatever your invention is, it ain't Frankenstein-cool.

You might consider not forcing non-employees to sign non-competes, unless they're intimately involved in product development. In order to make your non-competes and nondisclosure agreements stick (legally defensible), you have to provide compensation.

There are so many things to think about when it comes to operating agreements and plans. There are templates online that you can download for free. You can also ask your startup pals for help.

Check in with an organization called SCORE. They provide free services from retired executives, who will gladly kick your ass. These salty, seasoned consultants (although some of them suck) can be outstanding additions to your project teams and companies. The best ones will refuse to validate your hype.

If you're willing to curb your consumption of recreational drugs and reality TV, you can accomplish just about anything. If you commit to learning how to do it, you'll be able to cobble together excellent first versions of your operating plans and agreements. It might take a little time, but you can do it!

At the start of your venture, create your own operating plans and agreements. Otherwise, lawyers will siphon away your rent, food supply, health care and product development costs, leaving you in jeopardy.

 # Build Your Team

You need a strong team for your venture. Each member should have a title and set of duties. You can even make up fun ones like CDB (Chief Douchebag).

I meet lots of startups where everybody has matching hipster clothes, artfully trimmed beards and fascinating lexicons that make them sound like they invented something new, but nobody knows who's in charge or what the heck they're doing. These pretty boys spend most of their time arguing about the color of the logo and where to put their laminated Tesla poster.

Non-hierarchical hippie-style leadership sounds riveting, but it's nonsensical. In many of these cases, the CEOs are so passive and chill, their subordinates out-maneuver them all day long. These founders don't belong in the role of CEO. They should just get a job at a local coffeeshop and sell pot on the side. That's a better match for their work ethic and style.

Way too many startups list their team members but never tell anybody who is doing what. When investors ask them what the roles and titles are, they stare blankly toward the horizon. Nail these things down.

Titles and duties are also vital to operations. When people have titles and to-do lists, it's a tighter ship, it moves faster and you'll see revenue before you can say, "Why am I only making 8 bucks per hour?"

Your co-founders should understand the value of hard work. Some get so caught up in the imagined value of their ideas that they sit around fantasizing about how wonderful they are. Get rid of these folks early on.

Constantly cleaning up dead wood is a big part of running a startup. While turnover can't be avoided, you should always be perfecting your hiring techniques. If your front door isn't swinging from people joining and leaving the company, you probably aren't paying enough attention to what the startup needs and what these people are actually providing. Get comfortable with letting people go.

If your employees spend a few hours each day screwing around, that's a good thing. Just make sure that they're putting in solid effort the remaining nine hours. Yes, startups require a 12 hour work-day.

12 hours might be tough for millennials, who spend 85% of their time fantasizing and 14% discussing their fantasies over energy drinks. Then they need a nap.

If millennials are draining your bank account without delivering measurable effort, fire them. Then they'll have something to talk about when they're relaxing with their fake friends.

However, having millennials on board will bring profound advantages. If you treat them like partners, they'll be more passionate and more loyal than puppies. When their jobs are infused with a sense of adventure, their output triples.

Without a doubt, you will need other founders. I've met tons of founders who think they can do it all. They write grants, raise money, build products, and then screw it up because they didn't put the time into building a team with delegated duties. In order to show promise, you will need serious momentum. One person is never enough.

Limit the number of co-founders to no more than two or three. Make everybody else contractors who either earn stock or cash along the way. These folks don't have the same voting rights as founders. This keeps the paperwork simple.

When trying to figure out how much of the company each partner owns, be calm, cool and collected. If things get heated around this question, you might not have the best relationship with your co-founder, or you might not be well-suited for a startup. Relax.

At the start, determine an ownership structure that feels good to everybody. (Learn more about Cap Tables in the chapter titled, The Joys of Raising Money.) Remember that your startup isn't worth anything and your Big Idea means nothing until you execute to revenue.

Wondrous ideas and momentous startups die every day, largely because the company's founders spent money like foreign businessmen at strip clubs.

If you and your co-founders haggle about ownership for more than a few days, one of you is probably an asshole. To be fair, it's most likely you.

Do not micromanage because that will give you and your employees aneurisms. While aneurisms are exciting, save them for when you're a little older.

As your startup grows, you'll need high quality people around you in every department, because the more successful you are, the more scammers will emerge.

While once exploring a potential partnership, I found that the opportunity was much more complicated than I first understood. Assembling the facts into an easily digestible narrative, things became super clear: "A German man with a thick Russian accent, who has sporadic electricity and low-quality internet, contracted his close-friends as investors using lopsided legalese. Now, he's raising additional funds from "new" friends, who have not been apprised of how he blew through $350K on crappy legal work and a product he doesn't own or have the ability to access. All the while, he's doing business in countries where his premise is illegal, and claims that he might be out of touch for a few days because he's in the hospital with an unforeseen illness." I dropped him like a grenade.

As you construct your team and company, don't lie to yourself. Whether it's a candidate, partner, investor or board member, let the raw, unfiltered truth sink into your bones. Constantly be separating gold from clay and truth from hype. This will protect you from ever being owned or controlled by another person or entity. The truth will always set you free.

What about the folks who appear indestructible at the onset, but when things get tough, they whine like three year olds? You can avoid this by putting potential employees through processes of mutual discovery.

Invite them to the offices to hang out for a few days before contracting them. Give them meaty problems to solve. Ask direct questions about how they would handle specific situations. Engage them in mock brainstorms, discussions and confrontations.

Get under their skin and evaluate their reactions. Push their buttons to see how well they handle it. You might even spill coffee on them to learn about their first aid and burn prevention abilities.

While you don't want to go too deeply into the button-pushing arena, like sleeping with their spouses, set up scenarios during the interviewing period that provoke them to unveil pieces of their humanity.

Invite every potential employee to ask questions, take meetings at every level and join everybody for meals. This removes you from the equation, allowing them to explore the reality of your company so that they can make super-informed decisions.

You might even ask them to become a mock customer. This will teach both of you a great deal about your company's products, processes and culture.

Seek emotional intelligence in your new-hires and yourself. When people can empathize with other living beings, they'll always be encouraging and inspiring to others. If these new-hires are too shallow or unaware of how others feel, your warm-fuzzy startup can become a stale factory full of robots.

It's good to hire folks who make you a little nervous. Not because you think that they're dangerous, but because you get the feeling that their ideas could render you obsolete.

FunFacts

A pig's orgasm can last up to 30 minutes. *

US-based startups aimed at Finance, Insurance and Real Estate have the highest success rates. *

Investors are ineffective when they try to help startups. Sorry investors! *

Tech companies are the most popular startups throughout the world. *

The average startup closes its doors between the 15th and 20th month mark, after going through more than $1MM in funding. *

(*) FT.com, SmallBiztrends.com & Census Bureau's Business Dynamics Statistics, Brookings.edu, TechCrunch.com, BusinessInsider.com, Startupgenome.com, Startupxplore.com, Bootstrike.com

11 Negotiations & Incentives

When I was hiring people for our venture, the amazing Fred Silverman asked, "Now that you've done a comprehensive search, are you sure that you want these people on your core team? Do they have what it takes to hit home runs? If so, then pay them what they're asking. If you don't, then they'll find someone who will and they'll always be looking at the door."

A negotiated contract is only valuable when both parties experience a win. You might land a top-level beast, but if he's not happy, he'll eventually make you miserable. He might even exit upon receiving his bonus. Make sure every contract is mutually beneficial.

Do not enter a negotiation without knowing your bottom line. Do you ever Scuba dive without knowing your oxygen levels? Of course not. Always know your limits and be ready to articulate them.

More importantly, NEVER enter into negotiations unless you have the intentions, desires and ability to pull the trigger on a deal. Otherwise, you're just playing a game and wasting other people's time.

Some CEOs negotiate for months, for say, the role of paper clip holder. Unless you're negotiating a merger, drawing out negotiations is an outdated methodology. The average life of a startup is short. Be clear, swift and slightly aggressive in the push toward signature. Be alert for the perfect moment to stop negotiating. It's more of an art than a science.

If a negotiation gets too heated, you might feel the negative results of that heat for the duration of that person's engagement. If things get too complicated, do your best to give the favored candidates what they want, without hurting yourself.

When startups are driven by chaos, original founders can become needy and they can make hasty decisions. They might choose candidates who lied their asses off on their resumes. If you're not super-clear about a candidate's background, hit the pause button and do your homework. It might save you a meltdown.

Some new-hires will negotiate outstanding deals for themselves, but when it comes down to doing the actual work, they cave, complain or freak out. Make sure you grill a few references before making an offer.

Years ago, in my first c-level startup position, without realizing it, I hired a downright evil person into the venture. His personality was so sparkly spit-shined, I could barely see the real person behind the mask.

From day one, Dickie DarkSoul worked tirelessly to unwind my projects and dethrone me, all in pursuit of my job. To this day, he remains the most evil con-man I've ever hired. As a result, I learned how to maneuver around people who have bad intentions. I was patient, methodical and eventually won the game. While I hate games, if I'm forced into them, I become a medieval Wizard-King.

A big piece of every full-time employee or consultant agreement should include at least a stipend for healthcare. You might not be legally required to provide it, but it's your duty as a human being. Try not being an asshole like some of the schmucks pretending to lead the way in Washington DC and Silicon Valley. Everybody should have healthcare. Every single human being. It's a right, not a bonus.

Every employee and consultant agreement should include performance clauses that list bonuses to be received upon specific achievements. For every 1/4 point you award, make sure you've figured out what they will do in exchange. Every equity award must be a clear, mutually beneficial transaction.

If I'm to receive nothing in return, I hate to give away even 1% of equity. Meanwhile, I'll happily give away 20% if I'm to receive real value from that person, for example, new customers or additional funds raised. I like to award 1% of the company for joining the team and then up to 10% if they become rock stars.

I would also add "poor performance" clauses to your contracts, which should state the reasons for potential termination. There's a lot of dead wood out there and you should have the option to burn it.

Long ago, I helped fund a six-person venture and became their interim-CEO. The founder was a brilliant inventor who came up with a cool thingamajig. My job was to clean up the messes and get the company on the right track, which I accomplished.

The COO (Chief Operating Officer) was a young lawyer who I'll call Talky McDouchebag. Talky had manipulated this young, eager inventor into giving him 35% equity in the company, in exchange for incorporating and pleasuring himself at a few meetings.

McDouchebag had not simply negotiated a stunning deal for himself, he head-fucked the entrepreneur and pillaged the stock. The mistake that the entrepreneur made (prior to my involvement) was giving away too much equity in exchange for no value.

Within no time, I called McDouchebag on his bullshit and bounced him. He ran away like a coward and with ZERO equity. We were all so happy, we cried. It felt like we had lost a tumor.

There are con artists out there who regularly hunt down unsuspecting entrepreneurs. Their covert missions are to gain entry into cash cows and then suck them dry. If you're not careful, you'll make expensive, soul-draining mistakes. Be on alert for signs of manipulation. Not everybody has good intentions.

To put yourself in the best position, sit down with your founders and employees on a regular basis. Get to know them, even before you hire them. The more you learn, the better you'll be able to incentivize and inspire them. Find out what makes their hearts sing, and then find ways to help their hearts sing more beautifully.

It's easy to lose top talent, even leave before the 12-month mark, which is often when your investment in them starts to pay off. It's not always obvious why people become unhappy and leave early, but it's becoming increasingly popular.

Some people might slowly begin to despise themselves for the terms that they negotiated during a time when they had less confidence in themselves. It might also be that their bonuses didn't scale in a way that feels equal to what they had perceived to be their value. Someone's key motivators can be elusive!

Your company's office environment might tip the scales. While some folks love warehouse-style seating, others need privacy to be productive. Provide options.

Be innovative in how you lay out desks, dividers and social areas. Engage everyone in dialogues about how to make their work-lives enjoyable. Encourage them to play together throughout the workday. This will help turn your company into a home away from home. Check out the chapter entitled "Culture" to learn more.

Because many founders have never negotiated deals or hired people before, their cute, innocent startups can quickly become interpersonally cluster-fucked.

This happens when the CEO is so overwhelmed that he's unable to set aside ample time to get to know his team members, research potential employees and properly contract new executives and co-founders.

One of the most important questions you can ask a new-hire is, "What do you need to be effective in your position?" or "What would I need to provide so that you can become a rock star?" Some candidates might need 30-

person teams to be effective, while others will only need a whiteboard, an assistant and chocolate.

There are lots of levers to play with when bringing on talent. Not only is salary of value, but little things can sweeten the pie, like concert tickets, bus passes and gift cards. You never know what might tip the scale in your favor. In the process, don't be a carnival barker giving out cheap trinkets and toys. Strike an elegant balance will go a long way with your potential hires.

The biggest incentive that you can award your employees is your attitude. As the CEO or high-level co-founder, your vibrancy, encouragement, kindness and generosity will feed the hearts of your teams, your future and the future of your company.

Find quality people and get to know them personally before hiring them. Pay them what they're worth, then give them the support that they'll need to hit home runs.

12 Interns & Volunteers

There is nothing more important for your startup than bringing on a group of low-paid interns and volunteers. Not only will they save you money, but their efforts will take the edge off of insurmountable workloads. In return, you'll help them grow and influence their futures. To get interns for no-pay, their universities will most likely have to agree to give them course credit.

These happy-go-lucky youngsters are most likely smarter than you and your co-founders by a factor of 10. They'll have 10x the energy too. Without interns and volunteers it can be an uphill battle.

You might consider bringing on older interns too, people in their late 30's to early 70's. It's absolutely wonderful to have a variety of age groups running around the office. Everyone will benefit from the new relationships that they'll develop.

Seek the same diversity in the cultures, ethnicities and backgrounds of your employees. The more diverse, the more advanced your company's brain-trust will become. And please, PLEASE bring on lots of women. Women are better than men in just about every area.

You'll find that your interns will also surprise you in terms of their qualities and abilities. One of my interns was so brilliant that he's now running a Hollywood studio. Interns like these can be of great benefit to your business and might just save your ass.

Interns of legal drinking age are easy to enthuse too. Keep a tapped keg around and they'll love you forever. Get them tickets to insane concerts. Mentor them by taking them out to lunch. Introduce them to cute people in their age group so that they can get laid. Interns are the best friends you'll never have.

Interns and volunteers are like puppies. They'll believe you love them, even when you don't. And they'll surprise you everyday with their eagerness, open-mindedness and resilience. Simply by having interns in the office, you'll feel better about yourself, even when your co-founder is being a douche.

In addition to well-qualified interns who have interests in line with your company mission, hire a couple of folks solely for their radiant, engaging personalities. One vibrant captivating, sexy or charismatic intern can give your office a huge energetic boost.

Since not all magnetic personalities are able to inspire goodness in others, seek those who have kind hearts and can ooze positivity. Just by being their sparkly selves, they'll inspire others to rise to the occasion. By having one infectiously likable person in the office (with an undefinable job), everyone will feel happier and more confident. Everybody loves a mascot.

Plus, let's face it, most interns think about two things ALL THE TIME: their next party and who they'll want to have sex with at the party. Gone are the days when you pick people up at a bar. The gym is no place to find sexual partners because people are too focused on themselves. We find lovers and partners at work.

Give your interns real-world experience and mentoring. Help them to grow according to their passions and personalities. Don't phone-in the mentoring. Give it all you've got. Get to know your interns and make sure that they're getting value from you on multiple levels.

I was running a startup a few years back and we brought on 11 interns. We had a blast. They brought immense fun into the business. We had outrageous brainstorming sessions, enjoyed hilarious group lunches and we played after-hours drinking games often. These interns came up with innovative ideas and they kept us fired up, even when things were slowing down. I loved these interns and I learned a lot from them.

If your interns and volunteers ever have to quit because they found another job, they want to travel or because they got pregnant, make sure you give them a warm, generous exit. Why? Because for a few years, they gave you slave labor and you benefited like a plantation owner. Am I right or am I right?

Keep in mind too that college interns are sometimes super green, wildly unpredictable and horribly insecure. Some of them might require your parenting or older-sibling skills to keep them happy and motivated. While this aspect might occasionally be annoying, it'll feel good to help them. Remember how tough it was when you started out? Remember how many times you shit the bed? Keep that in mind when helping your interns.

You might also find a few healthy and eager volunteers at your local nursing homes. Heck, there might even be circumstances where you can safely invite a few homeless people to help out for a few hours, in exchange for free food.

Junior Achievement, The Boy Scouts, The Girl Scouts and local Boys & Girls clubs all have programs that allow teenagers to help local businesses in exchange for an education in how companies function.

Keep an open mind as you grow your startup. Find help where you can get it. Remember to be grateful for all the free labor. Your gratitude goes a long way!

Respect the time, effort and talent of every helper who walks through your doors. Shower each one of them with warmth, generosity and uncommon goodness.

 # Culture

The most enlightened and enterprising startups initiate discussions about company culture on day one. Why? Because culture has a huge impact on the products you build. Over time, your products and culture will live and grow symbiotically. They'll influence each other, kinda like BFFs or siblings on a good day.

A startup's culture consists of its values, beliefs and attitudes, which are built into the company's ideals, missions, visions, lexicon, relationship dynamics, work habits, processes and collective experiences.

Some startups are similar to religious cults, whereby a wacky, charismatic leader creates, controls and enforces a bizarre, restrictive set of ideals and rules through the use of secret handshakes, ancient symbols and t-shirts reminiscent of The Dharma Initiative. Even if they're benign, these complex, forced ideologies can feel oppressive, and will only piss people off. Yet even these cultures can be changed from within.

Keep in mind that truly deranged cults are led by egomaniacal leaders who use pain tactics, crafty manipulation and really bad Kool-aid to turn people into compliant, brain-dead lemmings. Chances are, no matter how colorful or restrictive your cultures are, you're probably not in any danger. Well, unless you work at Microsoft. In that case, you're shit out of luck.

Even though a startup might feel exclusive or cultish, its culture must be born from within and grown organically by the employees. If they own it, they'll embrace it and uphold it.

Long gone are the days when a startup guru could declare, "This is the way it shall be!" Elements of a culture must be discovered, explored and celebrated by everyone. It takes a village to create a culture.

You can't start a company culture with a memo: "Dear Employees at The Wacky Startup, We will now be recycling, meditating, buying kegs of probiotic beverages, brainstorming, engaging thought-leaders, playing foosball, innovating, politicizing, and believing smart things. If you agree, sign here _____."That just ain't gonna happen.

One of the first companies to create a unique and compelling culture was Ben & Jerry's Ice Cream. They were years ahead of their time. Not only were employees treated with a new level of respect, the company was set up in such a way that the CEO would never be paid more than 7x the salary of the lowest paid employee. This was unprecedented and gave the world a new model. You can read about this in the book, <u>Double Dip</u> by Ben & Jerry.

It's a noble mission to create a company culture, especially at a startup. With limited funding, creating a culture could be damned near impossible. With everybody stressed and war-torn, where will they find the time to worry about values and beliefs? They can barely find the time to pee!

It turns out that in challenging, poorly funded organizations, where peace, process and remuneration are scarce, culture is the elixir of life. Without a warm, positive, inventive culture, people might experience the startup and their lives as unbearable.

A company's culture can give people the Why they've always needed. A culture might have the ability to heal childhood wounds and inspire greater effort. While a culture can feed the hearts and minds of the employees, it might also save the company from ruin.

Here are a few examples of culture statements found in a culture definition:

1. *We will integrate fun into the work-day.*

2. *We encourage innovative thinking.*

3. *We encourage Socratic exploration.*

4. *We embrace diversity in every shape, color, persuasion & style.*

5. *Healthy food creates healthy minds. The mind gives life to creativity. We'll stock our kitchen with goodness. Healthy snacks, probiotic beverages and limited sugary garbage.*

6. *Exercise gets the juices flowing. We will each take time to get exercise, whether it's walking, running, hiking, biking or jumping up and down.*

7. *We will have non-gender-specific bathrooms because poop and urine are universal.*

8. *Crossdressing and flamboyance are not only welcome, they're encouraged.*

9. *Learning new philosophies of business and personhood expands our understanding of our world, our company and ourselves. We will have guest presenters and lecturers deliver speeches or workshops at least twice per month.*

10. *Napping is important to many of us. This is why we have (2) nap rooms, each with (2) beanbag chairs, (2) yoga mats and (2) cots.*

11. *As sexual exploration can free a person's mind and reduce stress, if employees feel like it and it is consensual, every person in the office is permitted to have sex in the phone booths, kitchen nooks, or on the non-cloth couches. The leather couch is off limits.*

12. *Work is stressful, so we will hire a masseuse twice per month to give free massages. Happy endings are extra.*

13. *We understand that some religions require daily prayer. We allow peaceful, religious expression at whichever times are desired by the individual. If your religion involves hatred or judgment against other people, please resign from the company and put yourself under house arrest. You should not be interacting with other human beings.*

14. *We believe in peaceful resolution through heart-centered mediation. We will have monthly trainings on communication and mediation techniques.*

15. *Peacefulness is a priority. If someone behaves like a butt-hole, it is okay to handcuff them to the radiator and throw grapes at them.*

16. *We are one collective, creative beast. All opinions are welcomed, as long as they are delivered with clarity and respect.*

Founders or other executives might use their titles or positions to enforce specific aspects of a culture, but in so doing, they might become the feared culture-bully, akin to the pushy control-freak on the playground who shouted, "It's my red ball. If we don't play my way, I'm taking my ball and going home."

If you have someone like this in your company, they might need your friendship, some gentle exercise, or oral sex. It'll be obvious which modality is best.

I was once hired by a startup to up-level their brand. The CEO was a lovely person with specific ideas around culture. Everybody liked him so much that they were afraid to hurt his feelings. This resulted in a culture of placaters. With widespread passivity, nobody would speak up about anything. The company folded within months.

Some people find little value in a company's culture, while others depend on it like it's oxygen.

Take your time building your culture. If you fancy another startup's culture declarations, try them on for size and see if your teams would enjoy adopting them. Or take it slowly, one step and one cultural element at a time.

The most important thing is to involve as many people as possible in the exploration and decision-making around your corporate culture.

Culture can inspire innovation, or it can push people out the door. Be careful with how you implement your culture. Your approach could produce the spark that creates magic, or it might be the spark that burns the barn.

 # Snacks & Nutrition

If you think you can get by with just a coffee maker and plain donut holes, you're living in 1973. If you're still pushing sugary coffees and chemical energy drinks, you might need a lobotomy.

In today's pro-health, pro-culture, pro-work environment startup scene, it's important that you consider your company kitchen as a key ingredient for winning over potential employees and keeping them healthy.

To compete in the startup kitchen kingdom and keep your employees from consuming chemicals, inject your kitchen with the most advanced and greenest products possible. I'm not just talking about salads, I'm talking about Moringa, Wheat Grass and Spirulina, the tremendous trio of toxin-killing powders.

A real startup kitchen doesn't have a Keurig. It has a spit-shined, award winning, Italian espresso machine, four local craft beers on tap, a bottle each of locally distilled Whiskey, Rye and Scotch, three on-tap Kombuchas, several little jars of powdered Moringa, Wheat Grass, Spirulina and Barley Grass, and a host of sugar-free, fake-sugar-free, chemical-free, vegan, protein powders, shakes and bars, each chock-full of insane levels of nutrients and antioxidants. You'll also want to stockpile organic chocolates, including ethically-sourced cacao and peanut butter cups.

Consider serving a free or discounted lunch at least two times per week. Don't just serve crappy, lifeless pizza or angry-cow, GMO burgers. Show the employees you care about their well-being. Make awesome meals!

Add nuts, vegetables and vegan options, plus veggie burgers, wild fish and organic meats. Have it all prepared by Buddhist nuns who chant mantras, or trained healers who can access the fifth dimension. You'll want these meals to be energetically optimized.

Why have all this variety and quality? Food affects attitude. Attitude affects performance. Performance affects your products and customers. Boost nutrition and everything improves, especially the bottom line.

Startup employees are connoisseurs of early morning beverages and afternoon snacks. When they're hankering for a hunk of organic minty cacao and an authentic Italian espresso con leche, guess what — they're going to pick their asses up and get some.

If they're working their faces off and need buzzes from local craft beers, guess what — they're gonna hit Main street and grab the beverage of their dreams.

Why not keep all this in house? This way, you don't lose employees and employees won't lose creative momentum. They grab a snack and get back to work.

Your developer might want to take the edge off his tweaked brain after crashing the servers AND the backup servers. What else would you have him do after an epic fuck-up like this? Sit quietly and meditate? Heck no!

Stock your cabinets with delights and your employees won't seek escape. They'll vamp on over to the kitchen, throw down shots of locally made whiskey, watch a little porn and get back to banging out awesome code. Am I right or am I right?!

Give people options. Variety equals employee retention. Food equals energy. If your food is crap, it won't provide lasting energy. If it's sugary, it'll negatively impact health and attitudes. Upgrade the food in your world and everybody benefits.

When you show care and love to your employees, they'll show care and love back. It's that simple.

Creating a healthy kitchen involves advanced thinking, open minds and the desire to source the most energy-infused meals, snacks and beverages available today. Food is life. Get to it!

Checklist #2

Bang out in under an hour:

- [ ] Start answering the questions in the Product Prep chapter (found at the beginning of this section).

- [ ] Write a simple Operating Agreement.

- [ ] Map out a simple Operating Plan.

- [ ] Write a list of incentives that you'll consider offering co-founders and key team members.

- [ ] Write your first vision for your culture.

- [ ] Post an ad for interns and volunteers on your favorite message boards.

Requires additional time and effort:

- [ ] Meet with the co-founders and key team members that you'd like to join your company. Enter into negotiations with the ones you find to be most impressive.

- [ ] Expand on the details or scope of work required to build your prototype or MVP.

- [ ] Expand, research and perfect your Operating Agreements and Operating Plans.

- [ ] Explore how you might incorporate meditation, peaceful walking, praycr, mantras, rituals and deep gratitude into your daily regimen.

- [ ] Practice being self-deprecating to keep it real.

- [ ] Choose one new sugar-free, nutritive, health food item to add to your daily diet.

15 Intellectual Property

Even though IP also stands for "Inpatient Program," like at a mental hospital, you won't suffer any brain damage if you file your own intellectual property using the USPTO (US Patent/Trademark Office) website. It's simple to use and it's inexpensive.

I submit my own trademarks all the time, and many other scrappy go-getters are doing the same. Ignore the legal thugs who tell you that you can't possibly do this yourself. Tell them to go fuck themselves.

After all, patent lawyers use doomsday speeches to sell fear for profit. They are the most expensive lawyers in the kingdom. If regular lawyers are Evil Overlords, patent lawyers are the Super-Devils who oversee all of the Evil Overlords. Fact.

For those of you who have sworn allegiance to your legal mouthpieces, keep in mind that hiring a lawyer to file your IP is very expensive, and it does not guarantee you anything — including being awarded your patent or trademark.

For under $1000 you can hook yourself up like a patent rock star. It takes a little time and effort, but filing your IP by yourself puts your discoveries on the map and saves you tons of money.

If your Big Idea is super-complicated, like a heart valve that also acts as a spout for olive oil, then you'll want to hire a patent lawyer or patent consultant to help you define every derivative of your inventions. Even if you hire one of these meatheads to outline your brilliant, Big Idea, you can still be the one who submits online at USPTO.

Set aside a week or two for learning how to submit your own patents and trademarks. Wander around the USPTO websites and familiarize yourself with the different legal terms. For example, "Amicus curiae," which means, "My friend needs to be cured of a deadly disease." This will surely come in handy.

After you learn all of the terms and create a product diagram or two, click on the links that lead you to filing your IP online. Take your time and read everything on that website. The US government did a solid job mapping it all out for you. It's just a little clunky in certain areas, similar to driving your old AMC sedan with the stick-shift on the tree. It's frustrating, but it gets the job done.

I highly suggest that you also read a book called, _Patent It Yourself_ by attorneys David Pressman and Thomas Tuytschaevers, the latter name having overtones of a hip new Scandinavian vodka. These guys provide a thorough education on filing patents by yourself on the USPTO website.

Once you've file your patents and trademarks, you'll wait anywhere from three weeks to 18 months before you hear from the USPTO offices with their questions.

If you're filing patents and trademarks before incorporating, put everything in your name. If you later form a company around your Big Ideas and its potential patents, you can give your inventions to your company through an "assignment."

With clear descriptions of your products, in every form and derivation, and with your company properly formed, you'll write an "assignment of intellectual property" agreement that states that you are giving your intellectual property to your company and that your company now owns the products and innovations you came up with, even if the patents and trademarks are currently in your name.

An assignment is a simple paragraph similar to, "The Wacky Cup Holder has an unusual big red handle. See our pretty diagrams in the attached picture, which also features my fiancé who is definitely hungover. We agree and are signed below stating that we are giving all of our Intellectual Property to our company named "The Cup Company" in exchange for one dollar. The Cup Company is now the new owner of The Wacky Cup product, images, concepts and all related intellectual property, including how the cup looks like a penis." Then sign the paper and put it in a drawer.

If you make a few mistakes when submitting your patents and trademarks, you can hire a patent attorney to clean up the mess AFTER you're funded. If you put the right kind of effort into this, you won't make a mess, unless you're like my friend Jimmy who continues to lose his keys in elevator shafts.

For some investors, patents are the most vital pieces of the pie. If you're claiming that your idea is truly unique, they'll want to see what the USPTO says about it. They'll want to know how defensible your Big Ideas really are.

The USPTO will reject an application for many reasons, including, for example, that you were high when you wrote it. In some cases, they'll give you a chance to amend your submissions and resubmit them. You may do so after you satiate your munchies and take a nap.

On the other hand, there are countless startup founders who believe that they just invented the world's first spoon. They spend all of their time paranoid that someone else may have already patented a derivative of their futuristic food scooper.

Before you file anything, research your patents and trademarks online. The USPTO website allows you to search current trademarks and patents using key words. This type of search brings up everything that's in process. At the conclusion of your search you'll know, with a fair percentage of accuracy, whether it'll be worthwhile to patent your unprecedented concave utensil or reduce the amount of pot that you smoke. Either way, it'll be illuminating.

Be reasonable about the value of your Big Ideas and whether it's truly worthwhile to file. Keep in mind, too, that large companies love to steal all sorts of things, whether it's your ideas, your money, your data, your life savings or your soul.

Defending your patents and trademarks is a whole other beast. This is when someone steals something from you and pretends that they didn't do it. The culprits are usually white guys in stiff suits. If one of these scoundrels screws you, you'll need some serious cash and a patent pit bull to bite their little balls off.

You might say that your inventions are "Patent Pending". This is savvy marketing in that it suggests that you have a secret that others cannot know. Milk this idea for all it's worth. Once the patent is issued, request for it to be unlisted (private), so that others cannot figure out how to "work around" your Big Idea.

Congratulations! You are barreling through this timely tome and you're almost halfway through the process of knowing how to become a global icon of industry.

Given your commitment to this book, I'm certain that I'll soon be spending $100,000 to dine with you, your entourage and your bodyguards, with the hope of bending your ear for a split second.

I look forward to bowing to your greatness and basking in your brilliance, if only for a fraction of a millisecond.

Learn how complex systems work. Trust yourself and put the necessary effort into improving your knowledge-base in the areas that promise to advance your business.

FunFacts

When you charge a fee for your product, traditional marketing (television ads, magazine and newspaper ads, newsletters, billboards, flyers) is more effective than social media marketing. *

Sea otters hold hands when they sleep to keep from drifting apart. *

Two of the most common causes of startup failures are self-inflicted wounds: Spending as if the company is in the Fortune 1000, and premature growth of operations without equal or greater traction in sales and revenue. *

First Lady Eleanor Roosevelt allowed only female journalists at her press conferences, ensuring that newspapers would have to hire women. *

(*) Udemy.com, Lyfemarketing.com, Adweek.com, BusinessInsider.com, ThoughtCatalogue.com, HuffingtonPost.com, BoredPanda.com

16 Advisors & Mentors

Open minds attract wealth. Surround yourself with mentors and advisors who are smarter and savvier than you are, and your startup will achieve a whole new level.

That being said, a crappy advisor might piss in your pool and make things incredibly difficult, not to mention, stinky. I had an advisor once who was just lonely. When seeking mentors and advisors, grill each one like you're running a private security company. Keep in mind that it's not actually legal to tie people up and pour water on their foreheads.

Your mentors and advisors are your triple-A ball club. They love helping people but they're itching to play in the big leagues as stock-compensated board members.

What's the difference between advisors and board members? You test advisors before bringing them onto your board. You drive them around the block, compare them to other advisors and then you pick one or two of them to sit at the big-kids table. It'll take some time to learn if they're worthy of being on your board.

Lots of startup CEOs patronize their advisors by yessing them to death, while rarely taking action on their advice. That's because it feels good to say yes. This is what little kids do. It's also enjoyable to change your beliefs and direction. If a brilliant person is giving you advice, listen carefully. Take it all in!

I worked with a startup CEO who yessed me to death for months. I had no idea that he wasn't taking any of my advice. It was disheartening to say the least. When his company gained momentum and attention, he was unable to handle it. He was afraid to bring on other founders and workers because he preferred chaos and control over teamwork and excellence. It was all ego.

How do mentors differ from advisors? There's a certain warmth to mentor relationships. Mentors are like moms, dads and uncles, (but not the uncles who drink too much and get naked at parties). You not only share your ideas and questions with a mentor, you'll probably begin to love them as well, even if they're tough on you.

Mentors help us to integrate our personhood with our business acumen. They help us to improve our beliefs, soothe our pains and encourage us to seek clarity. It simply makes sense to have mentors, even if they smack us around once in a while. That's their way of showing love.

After a few months of dating mentors and advisors, you might want to smack a few of them in the head, but you'll instinctively know if there's a board member in the mix.

To give the process greater clarity, be honest with yourself and ask these questions:

1. *Can I take direction from this person?*

2. *Do I admire and respect him?*

3. *Is their body odor reminiscent of a buffalo in heat?*

4. *Can she bring outstanding value to my startup?*

5. *Is it all toothless, sugary advice, or do they have enough confidence and brain-power to be candid?*

6. *Are they advanced enough in my company's sector and can I learn from them?*

7. *Does the sound of his voice make me want to punch his face or smash his laptop?*

8. *What meaningful introductions can she provide?*

9. *Do I believe the things that she tells me?*

10. *Can I show my full range of emotions to him?*

11. *Do I cower around this person?*

12. *When I meet with her, am I authentic?*

The last four questions are the most important. If you are unable to fully express yourself with someone, it means that you either unconsciously fear them or they have naked pictures of you cooking crystal meth. Either way, you'll resent them.

If you can't express yourself around your core team, advisors and mentors, your startup will suffer. To be secure and strong, always be authentic.

If you're too sexually attracted to an advisor or mentor, have sex with them first. If the sex is good, then it's okay to bring them on board. I'm kidding.

You want to be careful with sexual attraction. It can mess up business relationships like hot matches in haystacks. You have to be honest with yourself. Are you more interested in a joint venture with this person or would you rather see them naked in your kitchen, following 38 seconds of severe grunting? It's a crass question, but it's a vital one.

The most important aspect to consider is value. If there is limited value, then do not bring the person on board. If it feels more like a friendship than a mentor/advisor relationship, then be careful how you proceed.

I know a startup CEO who spends a lot of time taking meetings to validate her ideas, but she never capitalizes on these relationships. While these meetings make her feel better, her network is a giant support group. She continually seeks personal validation from faux, warm-fuzzy acquaintances, at the expense of the company. This is the not the behavior of a CEO.

For business relationships to be of value, they have to provide help that can be measured against customer growth and revenue. If your advisors are all feel-good cuddle-buddies and therapeutic coaches, you're being selfish. Growing your startup in the real world isn't warm and fuzzy. It can be downright painful.

Enjoy the pain. It might make you rich.

Three well-vetted, hard-won powerhouses will help you grow your startup faster and farther than a tree of luke-warm, milk-toast strangers.

 Networking Groups

There are many investor and entrepreneurial networking groups around the world. Some of them are prestigious and culturally diverse, while others feature large cadres of vain white guys, gathered in cozy circle-jerks.

The key here is to find groups that you both enjoy and that can be of value to you. Truth be told, you can waste a ton of time in networking groups. They can be bottomless rabbit holes filled with vampire muttonheads who'll suck the life out of you if you give them the chance. You must seek out only truly valuable people who you can trust.

Many of these organizations provide trainings, events and retreats focused on starting-up, investing in and sustaining businesses. Some of them provide real-world value, while others make you feel like it's Groundhog's Day, where they repeat the same events and the same sleepy themes every week, every month and every year. BIG YAWN!

Every worthwhile group has a special sauce, but they're only valuable if you have the time and energy to put into them, and if the members are of the pedigree that can advance your ideas, relationships and mission.

The cost to join these groups can be free all the way up to monthly payments equal to alimony. Be careful when you're asked to pay big bucks to attend local groups, especially the ones where members exchange little pieces of paper at the end that say, "Let's be in touch!" Let's not.

While these groups can be helpful to local businesses, their hefty fees are prohibitive. You'll never make that money back. Plus, you'll have to endure endless, long-winded speeches by sleepy insurance agents, phony investment advisors and robotic bankers.

These meetings make you feel like you visited The Island of Misfit Toys, on Dramamine.

Within every networking group, there are pretenders who dress like players, who'll only help themselves. They'll make you go through your presentation ten times, then they'll say, "Email it to me so that I can send it around." To whom? Your drunk golf buddies? Don't trust it.

These folks might just be hoping to bump into winners whose destinies they can control. To stop them in their tracks, just ask them if they have a Series 7 license. Without a Series 7, it's not legal for them to raise money.

If you like the person, just ask for personal introductions and promise them success fees. Most of these guys will disappear after they hear, "Series 7."

Below is a list of the types of people you'll find at most networking events. The first group are the folks to avoid, followed by the helpful folks who love to serve others. Obviously you'll want to keep an eye out for the gems.

FOLKS TO AVOID

The Siphon

The Siphon comes off like a munificent benefactor. He says all the right things, but when you scratch beneath the surface, you'll find that The Siphon only pretends to help others, and only if he's promised something in return. He might put himself on a panel for a startup competition, but will only vote for companies in which he's invested.

The Siphon will sneak into networking events to extract key players into side deals, thereby undermining the rest of the networking group's power. His only goal is to put money into his own pocket. You don't want this poser sniffing around your turf. Kick him to the curb!

The Idiot Marketer

He'll memorize a few facts about marketing, but has no experience. He'll offer free marketing workshops to startups, but only to later solicit the founders for business.

Pretenders like these have never actually run a real brand, except maybe a Cub Scout troop. They've never created traction for anybody but themselves. They're leeches who use hype rather than substance to initiate and control conversations.

The Social Whore

These are the wacky, friendly nut-jobs who run around networking events super excited, all the while making commitments that they never intended to keep. They'll pretend to be startup consultants, but these folks have no intention of doing any work at any time.

You might see the male version buying everybody drinks and making promises around "moving something forward." He might join your team for a few points in a deal but never show up to meetings. He's here to milk you for all you've got. The female version wears super low-cut dresses and uses her boobs as weapons. Her mini-skirts reveal so much of her private parts that you might easily read her lips. Ya know, the other ones. While some men fall all over this type of woman, she's a nuisance.

All Social Whores are really good at jerking people off and then disappearing. Even though ghosting is popular today, it often has dramatic repercussions.

The Unmanly Man's Man

You'll know this meathead by his 1950's lexicon and tight polyester suits. If he looks trendy, he picked it up from his son or "old man." His secret? He has no respect for women or femininity, except where he can capitalize on it.

Committed to preserving his caveman brain, he is unusually inappropriately non-inclusive. While it's one thing to be an equal opportunity offender, it's another to put men above women. Everybody knows that woman are more intelligent and more resourceful than men. Fact.

The Anti-Man Woman

This is a depressed or angry woman who has lost compassion and understanding for the men in her life, quite possibly for good reason. I have empathy for this person because society has been putting woman-kind through ringers for centuries. That being said, if you're going to be in a social network with 75% men, and on a planet that's 49% men, you might want to drop the chip on your shoulder and find the love. I understand that this can be difficult, but it's the best path forward. Being a victim attracts a great deal of attention, but it's very 1973.

It's always best to find forgiveness for the men (and everybody else) in your life. Forgiveness and being proactive are two of the most highly effective tools at home and in business. When we put them to good use, our lives are beautiful.

The Game Player

Game players are cancerous tumors that infect our lives and business networks with calculated, self-serving maneuvers. It's hard to identify game players, as they come in all shapes and forms. They use manipulation and coercion to serve covert agendas and they're dangerous to your business. Game players taint and pollute our connections to ourselves, our primary relationships and our lives.

While it's easy to hate game players, it's best to find compassion for them. On some level, they have no idea how disconnected they are from themselves, others and reality. They will never know the value of truth. There is nothing sadder than that.

THE GOOD FOLKS

The Investor Priest or Investor Priestess

The Investor Priests are sweet, generous and brilliant people who thrive on helping others. They see themselves as confessors who are able to help and heal the collective. These people actually exist and can be found in every startup networking group. You just have to know where to look and what to listen for. They generally do not advertise their quality, but they're open and available to be of service.

The Inquisitive Startup Lover

This inspiring and courageous person is always asking the right questions and always giving helpful hints to everyone she meets. With a well-balanced ego, she generously shares her ideas with enthusiasm. She'll infuse every conversation with light, intelligence, laughter and attentiveness. No matter the environment, she'll keep the flame going, always making you look and feel great. What makes this person even more wonderful is that she's 100% genuine.

The Eager Beaver

Every startup collective has a few of these super-newbies who are so excited to be part of a group, it almost feels as if they've been holed up in their moms' basements for too long. Even though they don't yet have much to offer, they're full of goodness and positive energy, Without a doubt, they are helpful additions to a network because they are the most innocent people in the room. They remind us of who we once were, a long, long time ago.

The Humble Connector

These folks are thoughtful and generous networkers. They're so successful that they rarely have to leave the house. With vast networks and deep pockets, they help countless people with referrals, guidance and encouragement. If you bump into these folks at parties, they'll grab your hand and run you around the room until you meet every person who could be of help to you. They are tireless, and they're always seeking to be of service, while asking little in return.

SUMMARY

We all have good and bad qualities. We are all selfish and we are all seeking to be of help to other human beings. I offer these archetypes as a resource to help you vet the folks who you hope to bring into your life.

There's a little bit of each of these personalities in everybody. Don't be afraid to see these archetypes as parts of you. This will help you identify these aspects in others. By mastering how you deal with each of these personas, you master aspects of yourself.

Endeavor to be generous as often as possible. Protect your company from selfishness. Improve yourself so that you can be a helpful, confident, powerful and successful leader. Set an example and you'll put yourself at the helm of the conversation.

Reject the twisted souls who promise you the world. Kick every knucklehead to the curb. Seek relationships with only positive, honest people. Embody peacefulness and network yourself to the bone.

If you join a networking group, make sure that you're in it not just for yourself, but to offer your skills, quality and mentorship to the collective. Be generous, loyal and of service to the organizations that you join.

Checklist #3

Bang out in under an hour:

- [ ] Determine (intelligent guess) which aspects of your products might have patent potential. Write short descriptions of each. Add hand-drawn sketches.

- [ ] Schedule individual meetings with eight to ten potential advisors and/or mentors.

- [ ] Follow-up with the ones you like the most.

Requires additional time and effort:

- [ ] Get onto the USPTO website and devour it. Become your own patent and trademark expert.

- [ ] Continually assess your advisors and mentors. Contract the ones with board potential.

- [ ] Research and join several entrepreneur networking groups. Attend their meetings regularly.

- [ ] Attend two startup events, meet-ups and/or presentations every week.

- [ ] Follow thought-leaders on LinkedIn, Facebook, Twitter and elsewhere.

- [ ] Research and learn about Cap Tables. Try to create one using the online template that you like best.

- [ ] Take your best friend and/or sweetheart out to dinner and tell them how grateful you are for their encouragement.

- [ ] Select a book from the Author's Favorites (at end of book). Finish reading it within a week.

Business Canvas

Your business canvas is the foundation of your success. It's a vital strategy tool that helps you formulate, outline and document each of the unique aspects, categories, levers and mechanisms that feed into your business model.

Every element in your canvas connects to other elements. It's hyper-comprehensive and it'll enhance everything you're hoping to accomplish.

Without a business canvas, you'll feel like you're wandering in a dark forest with a self-absorbed hippie who continues to lead you in the wrong direction. I can just hear your stinky hippie friend now saying, "Whoah compadre, but canvases are totalitarian buzz killers!"

I hear you brah, so why not create a canvas that helps you promote your idea to the people who can help you? You know, the ones who can write fat checks so you can move out of your yurt.

While business canvases can be a little intimidating, upon completing your first one, you'll feel as if you lost 50 lbs. and participated in a marathon. After my first canvas, I felt like I was on Ecstasy. It allowed me to see the beauty and connectivity inherent in our business. The canvas revealed all the magic that I knew was there. Even though I bled through the ears while creating it, it was worth it.

Without a canvas, you might only end up with a Fisher Price level business model. This might rock the house at Miss Mary's pre-school, but it'll fall flat when presented to accredited investors.

Don't rely on your grammar-school charm. Put in the effort to show your depth. Investors always know when founders are describing a fantasy born from ego instead of a premise proven via compelling research.

Champion your business model by mastering the following elements of a business canvas:

Key Partners

Your key partners are the active relationships that make your business function and drive you toward revenue. This includes individuals and companies that feed your business model. You'll enter into these partnerships to take advantage of new business ideas and relationship trees. Your key partners might also help you to reduce your own risk through the utilization of their readily-available resources. Key partners bring your business to life and help it to prosper. Without key partners, we'll steadily decompose. Examples of non-key partners would be your cousin Phil and that pimply teenager you hire to rake leaves and shovel your driveway.

Key Activities

Your key activities are the processes, actions and pursuits that support your business model. Key activities might include marketing, product manufacturing, service contracts, technology development, customer service and staring blankly into space.

Key activities probably do not include dating hotties, eating too much soy or congratulating yourself in front of a mirror long before you raise money or sell anything. If your business does not have key activities, it means your company doesn't do anything. This would be considered normal if you were a politician, but it's not normal if you're seeking capital.

Key Resources

Your key resources are the assets, talent and tangible services required to deliver your proposed value propositions (the reasons that your customers love you). These include buildings where manufacturing takes place, the tools and machinery required for product production, technology developers, sales teams, distribution networks and the cocaine that some people use to work through the night. Non-key resources might include your drug dealer Vinny and your former trainer who quit when you told her that sweating makes you uncomfortable.

Value Propositions

Value propositions are the attributes of the products and services that your startup offers, which hopefully solve problems and meet needs. Google says that it might include an "innovation, service or feature intended to make a product attractive to customers." You'll learn a great deal about your idea's value propositions through the process of building customer relationships, whereby you leave behind your gaming console and cheese doodles, and have meetings with verifiable human beings.

Customer Relationships

Customers drive your revenue because they pay your company for its products and services. There is nothing more important than establishing customer relationships. The more that you learn about your customers, the more you'll be able to serve them and profit from them.

Growing a tree of well-served, happy customers means your revenue will increase, unless you're selling lethal drugs, which tends to have variable, often declining, customer growth patterns.

Channels

These are the doors through which you push (distribute) your products so that they can reach consumers. You can interchange Channel with "Distribution Channel." It doesn't take ten distribution channels to prove your model. You just need one hot, proven channel through which customers purchase your products. This might be a brick and mortar store, a website or a sales team. If you're not adding Channels, you're not planning on selling products.

Customer Segments

Akin to customer demographics, these are sub-groups of customers, each one with distinctive marketing attributes, ages, genders, spending habits, interests, key words and locations. Keep this aspect simple at the beginning of your venture. A good example of a segment would be, "women between the ages of 18 and 25". A bad example of a segment would be, "People." If you segment too radically or broadly, you might become too spread out and never gain momentum with any of them.

Customer Pains & Gains

This is the Where, Why and How your customers suffer. Your job is to uncover the pain points that your products might heal. When you ask a question that makes your customers stutter, twitch or sweat, you've either struck a nerve or found something that causes her pain. Pain is your gold. If a product soothes pain, you make money.

Cost Structure

This is a list of your business's fixed and variable expenses that are incurred during the course of selling products. Many startups forget to explore every potential cost, which results in lopsided business models with insanely optimistic projections. Dig into the nuances of your expenses so that you can represent what it truly costs to run your business. If your business does not have any expenses, you might want to put down the hype-pipe and start watching business videos on udemy.com. Every business has a truck-load of expenses.

Revenue Streams

The most exciting thing about Revenue Streams is that they're positive numbers! Almost everything else is not. Revenue refers to the income that your company receives from customers when it sells its products. Some revenue has costs associated it with it. Examples of sales costs might be bonuses, marketing and Viagra.

Revenue streams are connected to a customer's pain. For every pain, there might be a unique product, and therefore a unique revenue stream, which would be awesome and attractive to investors.

Summary

Your business canvas and business model are interconnected sets of spreadsheets and algorithms that reveal how your business functions. If you can understand how all of the elements in these documents interconnect, you'll be prepared for when investors drive trucks through the holes in your thinking processes and assumptions.

To hit a home run, sign up at <u>InnovationWithin.com</u>. This is a comprehensive tool used for developing canvases. It will help you to connect the dots between Partners, Activities, Relationships and Costs. It also functions as an educational resource, guiding you through every step that's needed to create a compelling model. It's worth the money and it'll help you to become a better founder.

You'll be editing your canvas and model for months. You'll become so intimate with your model, you might scream its name during sex or Monday Night Football.

One of my favorite books is, "<u>Business Model Generation: A Handbook for Visionaries, Game Changers and Challengers</u>," by Alexander Osterwalder. Alexander also created a <u>Value Proposition Canvas</u>, which you can find online. This guy gets into the nitty gritty. Business is ALL NITTY GRITTY.

By mastering your business canvas and populating it with quality intel, you'll be more prepared than 90% of all startups.

FunFacts

Startups that track metrics, engage mentors and have founders who follow thought-leaders have 7x more money and 3.5X better user growth. *

Startups that pivot once or twice raise 2.5x more money than startups that fear pivots. *

Most toilets flush in E flat. *

When startups have only two founders, they raise 30% more money, have 3X the user growth, and are 19% less likely to scale prematurely. *

Cows have best friends. *

(*) Startupgenome.com, ThoughtCatalogue.com.
Boredpanda.com

 # Business Model

If you've built a comprehensive business canvas, congratulations! It will now take you 1/10th the normal length of time to build out your business model.

Build your business canvas and business model long before you hire a CFO (Chief Financial Officer). This will make you a smarter CEO and it'll put you in control of your financials, at least for the first ten minutes.

Once you've got your model up and running, you can hire a part-time (fractional) CFO to make it sing. When a model has all the bells and whistles that make investors drool, money and goodness flow to the founders, like rivers of gold from the Gods.

If building business model spreadsheets gives you facial nerve damage and chronic diarrhea, consider hiring a part-time CFO with whom you can build your first model together. This will empower both you and your business.

Whether it's you or a fractional CFO doing the work, extract every gem from your business canvas, then seek ways to represent those gems in your model. Remember, these two documents are interconnected.

To get cooking, you must learn a spreadsheet application, either Excel, Apple's Numbers or Google Spreadsheets.

Microsoft's Excel was a remarkable innovation when it first emerged, but filled with gaping holes. Apple took advantage of these holes by surveying Microsoft customers and uncovering a long list of their pain points.

As a result, Apple developed stunning solutions to this pain in the form of intuitively designed software and hardware. Every time I use Excel, I feel like it was created specifically to birth unalterable depressions and remove the beautiful colors from rainbows.

Digging in a little deeper, what the heck comprises a business model, anyway? A business model is a set of spreadsheets that outlines your revenue (the money your customers pay you) and your expenses (salaries, rent, internet, legal fees, condoms, marketing and other expenses that serve your business), resulting in an EBITDA (see below), along with a changeable, visual set of numbers that showcases how your company makes money, spends money and grows.

According to InvestingAnswers.com, "EBITDA is the company's **E**arnings **B**efore **I**nterest, **T**ax, **D**epreciation and **A**mortization. It measures the company's operating performance, without the inclusion of financing decisions (loans, interest rates, etc), accounting decisions (when and how your company spends money) or tax environments (the laws and jurisdictions surrounding how the government takes money from you)."

Startup founders who hate working on their financials pronounce EBITDA, "BLAH BLAH BLAH", but it is the crucial indicator of a business's ability to repay debt. Some CEOs call the EBITDA line, "Revenue available for debt service."

If you can answer these questions and if you're able to enter numbers into spreadsheets, you are well on your way to building a business model:

1. What products and services are you selling?

2. Your company real or is it a front for laundering cash?

3. What is the cost per $1000 to clean the cash so you can get it back on the streets?

4. How will you deliver or convey your products? What are the costs of delivery and conveyance?

5. What are the prices and levels for each product and service, in each customer segment?

6. What does it cost to sell to or contract your customers (i.e. the cost of sales)?

7. What does it cost to produce your product, or what is your COGS (**C**ost **O**f **G**oods **S**old)?

8. When home alone, do you enjoy running through the living room naked and dancing to Michael Jackson?

9. What are your labor costs (salaries, HR, etc)?

10. What are your actual costs for rent, insurance, employee benefits, utilities and Fruit Loops?

11. In terms of marketing, how will you find your customers? What will you spend to find them? What will it cost to incentivize and retain them?

12. After subtracting all of your costs, what is your profit margin (%) per sale, per product, per category, per customer segment, per year?

13. How does the resulting profit grow throughout one year and throughout four subsequent years?

Amidst doing all of this work, you might have a nervous breakdown, but you'll be the parent of a beautiful, bouncy, miraculous model. Woohoo!

If spreadsheets make you pimply, pale and anxious like a teenager on a first date, you're probably not cut out for the CEO role. Sometimes being the idea-generator is enough, and then it's time to get the hell out of the way.

Some CEOs are cute, quiet visionaries while others are hard-working beasts. Be truthful about your skillset and encourage the same in others. Poorly placed leaders results in confused products, timelines and processes.

As a founder, you can pick any title you want, for example, "Supreme Leader", but you'll eventually have to "work," as in perform activities that result in helping the company. "Work" might feel very different from wandering the halls and giving people high-fives. Just a heads-up.

If you can't live without the CEO title, you'll have to master business financials. This is a requirement of every serious, successful business person.

If you've never built a model before, you'll never be able to understand how you company is functioning. It's time to put your big boy or big girl pants on and build your first model. There are free courses online at SkillShare.com and udemy.com. Get to it!

Even though everything you do is wonderful, your first few rudimentary business models will not be strong enough to share with investors. If you show them your first model, they'll see you as a little kid running a lemonade stand rather than an investible CEO. You must perfect your model to the point of making a CFO proud.

There are thousands of business model books. My favorite is, The Lean Startup by Eric Ries. Dig into this book and take your startup to a whole new level.

Business models, also called Financial Models, drive your company's success and have the power to inspire potential investors. Be the master of your model. Do it now!

To be a great CEO, you must master every nuance of your business canvas and business model. Why? Because you'll be quizzed on them every day by potential investors and customers.

20 Executive Summary

An executive summary is a one-page document that details a down and dirty look at who you are, what you're able to sell, what you've done, what you need and where you're headed. It's similar to how resumes help you land interviews. It's the snapshot that investors need before they ask you to the prom.

If you plan on telling people about your startup, you'll need a powerful executive summary. This wow-document should be chock-full of perfectly distilled, compelling and truthful information.

Your "exec" should also be beautifully and intelligently designed. When creating it, never use fonts that can be found on promotional materials for kid's birthday parties, porn sites or Monster Truck rallies.

The executive summary is not about getting people to write checks. It's about landing meetings with investors, strategic partners and big potential customers. It's an introduction, a handshake, a kiss — but no tongue.

Some startup entrepreneurs pack 25,000 words into 8.5x11" sheets of paper, telling the reader everything that has ever happened in their lives, including stories about their first diaper. They use 3pt fonts that require 1000x magnifiers, along with special decoders used only by the CIA. Nobody reads these documents because it's physically impossible. The Smithsonian has several on display.

Tiny, overstuffed executive summaries make founders look like they're on serious medication. Be aware of what it feels like to read your document. It should be easily digestible, visually appealing and focused solely on your business, nothing else. Give investors and partners just enough information so that they will agree to seeing your 20-minute presentation.

Here are the key elements of an executive summary:

Company Overview

This is an enthusiastic statement about your company and its products, plus a handful of supporting facts and figures. It should read like the opening to a movie. It's the hook that compels the viewer to read the rest of the document.

This overview paragraph should be a bit of a tease, but not so obtuse that it confounds people. This is not the time to come off like an intellectual hipster. Be straight-forward and clearly outline the proposition.

Product

This is a clear statement about the problem that your product solves and the customers who might buy it. State the product's quality, its stage of development, pending patents and the status of customer traction. Close the paragraph with a statement that answers why this is the perfect time and perfect market for this product. Stay away from phrases like, "Brah, it's awesome, that's why!"

Market and Marketing Plan

Your market is the sector that your product fits into. It might be health, technology, sports, restaurants, tanning and home waxing kits. Clearly state what the primary market is and how you plan to advertise to your customers in this market. You'll want to be a little more specific than, "We're gonna tell all our brahs and stahs — and they're gonna be super-stoked, compadre!"

Competition

Identify up to three of your competitors along with how each of their products are compelling. Keep it simple, with no more than one simple statement about each one.

Also, describe how your product is unique when compared to your competitors. If you don't have competitors, you're probably high right now. Have a healthy snack, take a nap, and then come back to this one when you're ready.

Management

The management of your startup is the executive team that runs it, not its regular employees. Titles to include are CEO, CFO, COO, CMO, CTO, CIO and the like.

Titles not to include might be the designer guy, the part-time coder, and Awesome Bob who does that stuff nobody else wants to do, like deal with Crappy Tom. If you don't have all the title bells and whistles here, CEO is perfect.

Note three to four remarkable things about the CEO's career. Do not state that you and your founders are a "collective CEO." You need defined roles, otherwise you'll come off like a bunch of kids building a treehouse.

Funding Needed

A short statement akin to, "Seeking $350,000 in exchange for 20% equity in the company."

Financial Projections

Your financial projections are three lines excerpted from your business model that note the EBIDTA, revenue and expenses for the first three to five years of your company's projected growth. Keep this section super-simple.

Ancillary Elements

Add a picture or visual representation of the product. Along the top of the document should be the company logo and the CEO's contact information.

Make your document look pretty and keep the following ideas in mind:

1. Your Product paragraph should sing with the most beautiful voice on Earth. It should be short, sweet and inspiring. As an investor, if I feel huge waves of greed when reading this paragraph, you've done a great job.

2. Either in the Product or Market paragraph, state the problem, solution and customer segment. Inspire your audience by noting how your product solves problems and alleviates pain. Add a few facts and figures so that your readers get a sense that you have a fully functional brain. Truth matters.

3. State specific goals, limit the use of hyperbole and be specific. Drive people to your side with honest appraisals, facts and figures. Keep it real so that you can earn the reader's trust.

4. Polish your executive summary 20 times before you share it. Make it perfect. Be attentive to every detail, including spelling and grammar. You want to come off as if you spent $10K on it. Give it all you've got.

Too many startup founders run around with cartoonish levels of self-confidence and cringeworthy magnitudes of self-importance. They continually defend their blind spots and vulnerabilities, rather than consider the vital feedback that could help them improve. This is a form of self-sabotage and it's very popular in the startup world.

When startup CEOs become defensive, investors hear them say, "My massive, space-eating ego is far more important than listening to you wack-jobs." Be open and consider all the input that comes your way, so that you don't sound like you just had a lobotomy.

Most importantly, remain 100% honest. When you lie or portray false confidences, somebody will smell it. When you're transparent and admit your shortcomings, you tell the room and the universe that you are humble and trustworthy enough to receive investments from strangers.

Admit that you have questions and blind spots, then engage advisors, mentors, co-founders and key team members to help you turn your deficiencies into strengths.

Your executive summary should be flawless.

Seek counsel that helps you to assess every aspect of the documents you share publicly.

Don't skimp on preparation or truth.

21 The Presentation

When you have well-researched, engaging and timely presentations, and you can deliver them with confidence and enthusiasm, you'll vastly improve your chances of raising capital. If you haven't been blessed with the gift of gab, consider hiring a charismatic co-founder to be the new company mouthpiece.

If their presentations are well-researched and intelligent, emotionally expressive, openhearted people can change a company's future with one speech. With all of her sparkly charm, a charismatic founder might also receive most of the attention, which will give you gobs of free time. And just by association, they'll make you and your team look more attractive. It's a win-win-win!

Having engaging mouthpieces for your company is not about the spin or sex appeal, it's about their ability to infuse the hearts of your audiences with light, causing them to be more open, more authentic and to come alive. This increases receptivity and invites success.

Whether it's you or the new face on stage, make sure your presentations serve up substance rather than flash. Depth and complexity is vital. To raise money, you must build a profound, inspiring and comprehensive presentation.

Many startup CEOs can bang out a smoking hot presentation in under three hours. They do this by combining their hack-design skills with their compulsive research abilities. They push and push until they give birth to a presentation that sings.

The rest of you, I'm sorry to say, are presentation-challenged. You'll need to copy designs from someone else and trudge through the research. You must learn how to use Excel and PowerPoint immediately.

If you're game, try Apple's Numbers and Keynote. They're light years ahead of the comparable Microsoft products and more enjoyable to use. The more you enjoy the process of making presentations, the more engaging the materials you'll create.

Whether you're the CEO, CMO or the Product Manager, be sure to turn on your beautiful heart-light at the start of every presentation. This will awaken every sleepy or dim-witted soul in the room.

There are a lot of opinions out there about how many slides you need in your startup presentation. A good rule (that won't stress you out) is no more than 25. If you can trim down to between 12 and 20, you've done well.

There are hundreds of stunning, powerful decks online. Find design templates that you love and copy them.

Below are the slides that you'll need to create for your flawless, vibrant presentation. Make each slide pretty, concise, engaging and easy to read.

You might make a few versions of each slide. The more presentations you do, the more you'll be able to assess which slides are more effective at getting the points across.

1. Elevator Pitch

This is the most enticing, exciting thing that you will share about your business. It should be brief and no longer than 20 words. The format might be something like: "Company helps Customer fix Problem because of This Pain. Market opportunity is $Billions. Current traction: 1312 paying customers." Refrain from hyperboles like, "We're going to be the next YouTube!" since that will make you sound like you have brain damage.

2. Problem & Solution

What are the pain points that your customers most complain about, related to your product or service? How are you approaching these problems? How does your product heal or solve one or more of your customer's pain points? Illustrate how your product is the perfect match!

3. Product Overview

What are the attributes of your products? How are they delivered to customers? What is the pricing?

4. Market Size

Your market size is the total number of people (broken out into customer segments or specific groups) that your product serves.

5. Business Model

This slide illustrates how your company forms partnerships, makes money, spends money, scales (grows) and increases profits. This slide separates the potentially fundable startups from the ones run by bearded, pretty-boy founders who grow pot in their kitchens.

6. Financial Summary

This is a four-row, five-column spreadsheet that denotes Revenue, Expenses, Contingency and EBITDA, across five years. This is yet another slide that separates the successful startups from the ones where the founders repeatedly give themselves high-fives and fist-bumps throughout the day.

7. Competition

Outline three primary competitors, the product attributes that you have in common, and the attributes that prove that your product is a cut above the rest. If you don't think that you have competitors, you're drunk.

8. Go To Market Strategy/Marketing Plan

These documents outline how you'll get your product out to the masses upon proper funding. State the costs and concepts that will drive customer discovery and outreach. List your marketing channels (Google ads, Twitter ads, etc.) and every cost related to marketing.

Calculate the average one-time and average lifetime values of your customers and state your marketing's return on investment (ROI).

Research the most recent trends so that your plans and strategies are continually up to date. If your current marking strategy is to drink beers with bros and hit a few parties, you might need some education in this area.

9. Team

These are the key executives and founders who run the day-to-day operations. Include four bullet points about each person. Add a slide showing your advisors, mentors and partners. Don't add slides with pictures of every employee, intern and contractor, otherwise your presentation will look more like a dating app.

10. Traction/Projections

State your financial projections and include a graph that illustrates your revenue projections. Consider adding a few of the mind-stimulating calculations that investors often hope to see. You can list the following calculations in the upper right hand corner of your graph:

- *If we raised $X, it will allow us to grow an annual revenue of $Y.*

- *Our runway (number of months until we go broke) is Z number of months.*

- *CAC (Cost to Acquire Customers) is established by looking at how much money it costs to find a customer (often, your marketing costs), including the dinners you buy when kissing their asses.*

- *LTV (Lifetime Value of the Customer) is calculated by looking at how many times an average customer will buy your products. An equation for your LTV might look like:*

  - *Our average customer will purchase our product 12 times per year, at $5 per month, for an average of 3.5 years. The LTV in this case is $210.*

- *MBR (Monthly Burn Rate) is how much you spend every month (not including beer, pot and condoms) to keep the company alive. Your MBR takes into account every expense.*

- *MRR (Monthly Recurring Revenue) is the average amount of money that your company receives from paying customers every month.*

    - *Calculate this by adding up the past six months of revenue plus the revenue you're projecting over the next 12 months. Your MRR is the average of the sum of these months. If you have no revenue to date, just make this shit up, but base it on real, honest-to-goodness research.*

11. Exit Strategy

No matter how charming you are, investors will not want you to run your company for the next 50 years. No matter how long you've been distilling your own whiskey, nobody wants to be your partner for more than 48 months. Your Exit Strategy is a graph or list showing who might buy you, why, when and for how much.

Research the types of purchases and investments that your potential exit buyers regularly afford. If your plan is to go public (IPO), be clear about the valuation and the timing. Make the Exit Strategy so epic so that it inspires investors to Friend you, Like You and put you on speed-dial.

12. Needs

This outlines the positions and key expenses that will help you expand. For example: Chief Marketing Officer, Sales Director, Lap Dance instructor and marketing expenses. When outlining your Needs, consider the roles and expenses that pave the quickest paths to revenue.

13. The Ask

The Ask is how much money you are raising and how much equity in the company you are willing to give away for that amount of raised capital. Unless you've been asked to NOT include this slide, investors will want to see this.

Be prepared for pushback on this slide. Pushback is when investors say, "You're not asking for enough cash", "Your valuation is too high", or "You're a putz.". If they challenge you beyond your comfort zone, this is a great time to demonstrate composure and confidence. If they ask you a tough question, only say "Fuck you, asswipe" in your head.

14. Closing

This slide should include five highlights about your startup. Each bullet should be ten words or less. Put this slide on the screen as you're being introduced and again at the end, so that it's on the screen during the Q/A period.

After you present, be ready for questions about your models, projections, assumptions and weird hipster t-shirt. Smart investors will ask you how you arrived at your numbers. Be honest and don't freak out. If you don't know something, say, "Let me get back to you on this one".

Research

There are many places online where you can pay for research to fill out your business model and improve your presentation. Forrester (https://go.forrester.com/) and D&B Hoovers (http://www.hoovers.com/) are two of the best. You'll be able to find heaps of information online for free. Have patience and dig deep. You should rarely have to pay for research. Libraries are also quite remarkable.

Presenting

Be passionate, confident and take your time. Do not race to the end like a crazed crack-devil on amphetamines. Do not rehearse by presenting to friends, unless there are also CEOs, investors or advisors in the room. Otherwise, you'll get a long list of conflicting notes from people who can barely dissect an episode of The Simpsons, let alone the metrics required to label a startup as fundable.

Finally

Be prepared to create multiple versions of your presentation, each one catering to a unique audience. You will also want to have presentations for every time-slot length that you might find at startup events, including lengths of 5, 10 and 20 minutes.

Investors are usually pretty straight-forward. They want to know: 1) If you and your **Team** can execute. 2) If your **Solution** solves a real **Problem.** 3) If the **Market** is valuable and if you understand it. 4) If you know your **Financials** and are able to plan and budget like a pro. That's it! If you can successfully inspire confidence in these four areas, you'll be a contender.

It might sound silly, but be sure to enjoy delivering your presentation. Be yourself! Your love for your company will be infectious. Dress up like a pro and go get em, Tiger!

Continually improve your presentation by pitching to advisors, mentors and industry professionals. Regularly update your research. Stick to the facts. Limit the hype. Graciously consider all feedback.

22 Scaling Fantasies

Some founders will attempt expansion into new countries, even before they have one sale in the US. That's like buying land in China before you can afford an apartment in Jersey. Just to be clear, I love Jersey.

Scaling too soon is one of the primary reasons why startups fail.

I've met amazing CEOs who wait for specific triggers before wandering outside their own zip codes. They'll hold out for improved traction, decreased marketing costs or for their oldest executive's long awaited sabbatical, before allocating funds to new regions.

I get it, it's exciting to love your startup. You want to tell the world about it, just like the time you made out with your high school chem teacher. It makes sense that you'd want to break free and shout from a mountain top. The problem is that expansion requires money and resources, which most startups won't have until, well, maybe never.

I once worked with a CEO whose startup had an incomplete product and only $10K in the bank. In his infinite wisdom, he thought this was the perfect time to hire five full-time sales people and buy them matching golf clubs. Cocaine, anyone?

We finally reeled him in, but was he deranged? No, he was your average newbie with no internal reality-check. Could his actions of offering full-time positions, with no money in the bank, constitute fraud? You betcha!

To run a successful startup, you have to suppress your ego at every turn and adapt your plan to every piece of intel. If the intel doesn't point to surplus, you can't expand. In most cases, you'll want to get a hobby and sit tight.

Even though you can't afford to scale, you'll still need to illustrate the scaling potential of your model, otherwise you won't get funding. This is because your investors need to see that you'll *eventually* blow the doors off the market. Keep in mind that they love profit more than they love themselves, and almost half as much as they love Viagra.

Make sure you rapidly and regularly perfect your product so that your early adopters stay in love with you. You'll want to make these people consistently super-crazy-happy BEFORE assuming the rest of the world will follow suit. It might be that your success is a fluke, all based on that wild, naked weekend you had in Key West.

Consider when the The American Dairy Association invaded Mexico with their famous slogan, "Got Milk?". Translated into Spanish, this equated to "Are you lactating?". Don't be the crazy drunk guy who wakes up the next day regretting that he bought a bottle of Cuervo for every person in the bar. Gracias, señor! De nada!

Do the research! It might appear that Iceland is your product's perfect first market, but refrain from making jumping into that market just because it's cold, they like to cuddle and they speak perfect English. It might be more profitable if you translated, rebranded and launched in Asia, simply because they love rice. Test, develop, test, develop, test, and then test some more!

Consider too that it's difficult hiring and incentivizing employees in other countries. You can't learn how to motivate a Brazilian just by visiting a Motel Ocho in San Paolo. You need to crank out some serious analytics so you can learn how a culture and its unspoken systems work.

Whether it's Mexico, Canada or South America, every country has its own unique identities and styles. Russians are so harsh, you'd think that every interaction was a physical battle. Chinese are so critical, you might hate yourself after working with them. Indians are so warm, you might prefer their friendships over pushing them to complete their work.

American ex-pats and those on US soil are the worst. We're either arrogant or grumpy. While Croatia and the Philippines are catching up, America is backing-up.

Slow down and push to recurring revenue. Without it, you'll look like an idiot — like that time you let your sister cut your hair in her Barbie's Magic Hair Salon.

You don't need to cross an ocean or even a state line. Your fans and customers are right next door.

If you push too far and too soon, you'll burn through cash and good will.

You cannot scale your way into profitability.

23 The Pivot

Just when you've got it all nailed down, a hurricane blows in, fills your boat with what-the-fuck and pushes you in strange new directions. Are you going to fight the tide? No. You're going to rebuild the boat, chart new territories and pivot like a wild, savage Viking! To be clear, I'm a big fan of Vikings.

Change ain't a bad thing. Statistics tell us that most startups have to pivot to remain alive and competitive. A well-timed pivot can save your company and hair line.

When all of the intel points to changing the product or segment, just pivot toward the numbers. Do not pretend that you're the All and Powerful Oz. You're more like Dorothy — tired, vulnerable and in need of a home.

You want to be careful not to pivot too soon or too much. Sometimes, it's about sitting around in wet underwear and riding out the storm. Be sure to weight all of the information at your fingertips and seek counsel from experienced advisors before you flip the switch on change.

A pivot is an organic, necessary change in direction. Pivots usually don't happen by choice, most often they emerge as obvious options after painful events, like a loss of market share, low sales, or he cheated on you with that whore-bitch in Minnesota.

Some CEOs fight pivots up to the point of the bank seizing their dentures. You can't blame a CEO who self-indoctrinates to the point of fantasy. Once we get attached to a path or ideology, it's difficult for any of us to change. But if you're not looking out for pivots, you're not a CEO.

I once helped a startup who sent me to Asia to source technology customers. After 31 (really) meetings, I found the perfect partners for us. It required a huge pivot, a joint venture and slicing up our platform to make it all work.

When I pitched the idea to the CEO, he spent 20 minutes ranting about the value of his original vision, but then he said, "This is an excellent opportunity to pivot. Let's do it!" When CEOs deflate their own egos, it can be life-changing for their companies and employees.

Whatever your product is, you are most likely not fully aware of its niche, customers or long term value. The truth about your venture has not yet revealed itself, like your wife's orgasm. The brilliance behind your original Big Idea is still percolating, and it'll be percolating for a while.

The same goes with your corporate message. Sometimes you have to change your marketing, tagline and product names to inspire customers to bite.

I was a spokesperson for a company a while back and I created a comedic, educational presentation for their global partners. While touring the world presenting the show, I became aware that one of their products had a Chinese-sounding name that could be translated to "Cow gives birth with fat smile." This was not flattering.

When I shared my concern with the smarmy CMO, she said I was paranoid. Two months later they fired her and changed the name due to pressure from investors. Had she been a little less distracted by her distorted self-image, she'd have saved the company $300K in PR, marketing and branding, in addition to a ton of brain damage.

A pivot can happen at any time and in any category. It might include more than just products or messaging; it might take out a few individuals or teams. These are the hardest pivots to make because they involve firing people who depend on you or people you truly admire.

You might pivot from one business sector to another, simply because your current sector is a pain in the ass. For example, schools and governments tend to drive startups a little crazy at first. This is because they're similar to McDonalds, with franchisees in every city. This can be overwhelming to take on.

To succeed in these sectors, you're forced to sell to each individual office, each one with their own unique hierarchies, rules, games, politics, processes and machiavellian villains. Pursuing these sectors also can cause migraines, Cat Scratch Fever and Maple Syrup Urine Disease. If you're in a no-win situation like this, where you're banging your heads against a wall, pivot.

If you're entering sectors that stretch beyond your experience, be aware that there are dangerous crooks who can smell your pretty, fresh meat a mile away. They'll do whatever it takes to bring you to your knees. They've been waiting for someone like you for 10 years.

What if your product pushes customers too far outside their comfort zones? I know a brilliant inventor whose company built 25,000 aluminum electrical gadgets. It wasn't until they went to market that they learned that the electricians who would install them would only use steel. This is why customer discovery is so important.

Your product might only need a subtle pivot, with a change in color, tagline or description. My friend Barry Wolfman, who owned a high-end pizza chain on the east coast, said that when he added the simple tagline "Owner's Favorite" to his most expensive pizza, its popularity jumped from #12 to #2. Before you toss out a whole pie, seek out simpler and less costly pivots.

Pivoting is about being in the moment and being honest about what you are experiencing. It involves listening with both your mind and your heart. Together, your mind and heart comprise your gut. If you continually listen to your gut, you will always know exactly when and how to pivot.

Don't hang onto disasters just because you almost killed yourself bringing them to life. Let go, pivot or start again.

Checklist #4

Bang out in under an hour:

☐ Select your favorite business canvas template online and create a gut draft in under 20 mins.

☐ Quickly build a rudimentary business model in under 30 minutes.

☐ Research and make a list of the titles for your presentation slides, with no more than 25.

☐ Hunt down a template and structure for your executive summary.

Requires additional time and effort:

☐ Reach out to SCORE for free seasoned help.

☐ Dig deep into your business canvas and business model and make them stronger.

☐ Consider signing up for online services that can help you perfect your canvas and model. For example, InnovationWithin.com.

☐ Research, create and/or select a clear, simple design for your presentation.

☐ Create a first draft of your presentation using your list of slide titles. Don't overthink it.

☐ Spend a full day working on perfecting your presentation (your deck).

☐ Dance naked in your living room for two full songs.

☐ Say "I love you" to three people, preferably people you already know, so as not to freak anybody out.

24 The Joys of Raising Money

When someone gives you money to fund your dream, it's a remarkable moment in your life. It feels as if all the forces in the universe conspired to support you. It's as if you're invincible. There is nothing quite like it.

Taking on serious investors can also be overwhelming. To prepare yourself, brush up on Cap Tables, Dilution, Revenue Shares and all the forms of investor agreements. I'll outline a few of these key points to get you started.

When an investor buys into your company, you give them a percentage of the company in the form of stock or shares. If there are investors and other stock holders already on board, then everybody is diluted (reduced) by the percentage of stock the new investors are promised.

Your list of investors and how much stock each person or entity owns is called your "Cap Table," short for capitalization (i.e money). A capitalization table is the breakdown of founder, member and investor ownership percentages and how these values dilute upon future rounds of investment.

You can find Cap Table spreadsheets online. Don't be afraid to explore this topic. With a little time and effort, you'll be able to rattle off a Cap Table in no time.

As an obsessed startup founder, you'll always be wondering how much equity you still own — a number that will haunt you, and cause erectile and vaginal dysfunction until the moment your company goes public.

Remember, if your company is not making money or if you only have a few customers, your stock isn't worth a half-cup of walnuts. Be reasonable when investors nibble.

How do you find investors? Check out the chapters titled "Networking Groups" and "Accelerators & Incubators".

In the meantime, here are some additional tips:

1. *Find out where they live so you can camp out on their front lawns.*

2. *If you know where they work, wait for them outside, then jump out and yell, "LOVE YOU MISS YOU!"*

3. *Send them Linkedin messages every 10 minutes.*

4. *Sit behind them at events and stare at them.*

5. *Invite them to a men's bath house.*

Feel better now? You're welcome. There's no magic to finding investors. Network, go to startup events and reach out to friends and ask for quality introductions.

When forming relationships with investors, be aware that there are 1000 other invention-obsessed lunatics trying to grab their attention. Investors are people, too, so be human with them.

Some entrepreneurs will turn psycho, latching onto investors like industrial vacuums. Let go and breathe. Instead of pushing investors to critique every shit you take, how about getting to know them? Ask them questions like, "How's your day?", ya know, like a human being.

Keep in mind that investors are not magical angels seeking to fund your dreams because they love you. They're skilled marksmen in pursuit of deals. They want to be in business with you because you proposed a low-risk investment in a way that inspired their confidence.

Every investor and firm is looking for the next Facebook, or at least a startup that models a 10x exit within three years. What is a 10x exit? It means you're AWESOME. It suggests that your business model (how your company makes money) creates so much wealth that investors will earn ten times their investment in a short period of time.

Investors can be tough, sometimes nasty. I've heard several hilarious, albeit evil responses to entrepreneurs IN THE ROOM, seconds after the presentation. These are the most fascinating punches in the groin that I've heard investors say directly to entrepreneurs:

1. *Are you solving a real problem here, or are you just jerking off?*

2. *You should be more like Uber.*

3. *The money you've put into your startup doesn't qualify as an investment.*

4. *I like your idea, I just don't believe that you're capable of executing.*

5. *When you hit $100K monthly recurring revenue, call me!*

Sometimes investors will say bad things about you one minute after you leave. Here are a few gems that I heard moments after the entrepreneurs left the room:

1. *Well, that's 15 minutes of life I'll never get back!*

2. *Did that mind-numbing catastrophe actually happen? Or did somebody plop a mickie in my latte?*

3. *We already had that idea, didn't we? (Evil laugh.)*

4. *I wish she was dressed more like a human than a cartoon character. And I wish she was prepared.*

5. *No market slide, no problem slide, no team members and no ask. What did he expect to happen here, bro time?*

If an investor says something mean to you, it's about them, not you. DO NOT become defensive when they rattle your cage. Stay calm, cool and collected. This is what real CEOs do. Take the hit, let it flow and come up with a thoughtful response. Never react in the moment, unless you can respond with authority.

Sometimes investors use verbal abuse to test an entrepreneur's resolve. This is because they only want reasonable CEOs who have the self-confidence to remain calm and respond intelligently, even in the face of abuse.

If the investors become abusive, here are a few things you could say to put them in their place, but resist the urge:

1. *What was your college major, dream demolition?*

2. *When you first fell in love, was it with yourself?*

3. *Where did you lock your inner-child, in your inner-basement?*

4. *How many times has your wife left you?*

5. *When did your soul become a revenue center?*

Some entrepreneurs don't realize how lucky they are to have investors. Moments after they move into their investor-funded offices, they begin to resent how much equity that they gave away. This leads to taking their investors for granted. Investors aren't always the easiest people to deal with, but they were there for you when you needed them, weren't they? The only way to return the favor is to be loyal. This is a rare quality today.

Some might even say that you're their bitch, but is that really a bad thing? Bitches are powerful and fiercely independent, which are helpful attributes when pursuing a dream. Call me a bitch any day.

I was advising a startup that showed great promise. The CEO sounded as if she knew her product and market. What her board later learned was that she was hemorrhaging money like a teenager, flying around the world hiring new people, with barely a dime in the bank. Not only did they advise her to refrain from further travel, they told her that they were alarmed by her overspending and lies. Yes, at some point, hyperbole is lying.

At first, she refused to negotiate and threatened to fire key board members. Eventually the board called for a healthy sit-down, upon which she acknowledged her mismanagement. The board then infused the company with capital and she continued without a hiccup. Some founders find it difficult to admit to having blind spots.

Here are three simple but crucial take-away lessons:

1. Never kick your supporters off the ship, especially your investors, who are your primary lifelines to future capital. No matter how tough people are, keep everybody on the ship. That's what great CEOs do.

2. Never run away from a deal. Sit confidently at the table. There is always room to negotiate.

3. Be grateful for the people who have invested in you. Seek counsel from them. Ask them for help in areas that challenge you. Heed their advice.

When you reach out to investors, they'll want to see your executive summary, which you should have prepared by now. If need be, reread the Executive Summary chapter.

I've met some super-cocky, control-freaky startup CEOs who tell me that while they don't have an executive summary, they would like to meet me in person so that I can "experience" their one-hour presentation. Um, no.

If you require every potential advisor and investor to sit through your precious, unedited presentation, equal to the length of *War and Peace*, you must be mainlining heroin.

Enduring first presentations that are longer than 20 minutes is akin to being waterboarded. Be humble with regard to your Big Idea, an idea which may or may not be unique, valuable or interesting to anybody but you. 20 minutes is long enough for a first meeting.

If you're a startup founder and you're telling investors what length of time they should allot in order to fathom your concept, you're an unaware, self-absorbed putz.

The remedy here is to SLOW DOWN and get over yourself. Get your presentation ready and take every meeting that you're offered. You need practice.

Some super-newbie startup CEOs demand that investors sign NDAs (non-disclosure agreements), even non-competes before they'll present or share their executive summaries. These documents are not enforceable unless people are compensated, ya know, paid money. And unless you've found the cure to cancer or invented a process to put terra-forming into a can, give it a rest. Even MDNAs (mutual non-disclosure agreements), where neither party can say anything about each other's shit, can be overkill.

As you grow your investor team, do your best to retain the voting majority for as long as possible. Some investors might even be open to giving you their proxy, where they have no vote and your vote counts more than once.

You're lucky to have a Big Idea for a startup, and you're lucky to have investors that are interested in speaking with you. Remain grateful and continually improve your presentation, education and attitude.

With a little luck, you'll present to a crowd of ripe investors who will infuse your company with $1MM cash and then continue raising money for you, all the way to your Series A, B, C and D. That's when you'll be taking all of your meetings in your pajamas, while atop that beautiful mountain peak on your majestic new island.

Keep up the great work! You're moments away from building the world's first gold-plated, underground survival shelter and employing the largest harem of personal servants since alien Egyptian Gods roamed the Earth. Prostrations to the all and powerful YOU!

Never tell investors that they need to spend an hour with you. Any investor worth their salt can vet you and your idea in 10 minutes.

Find Accredited Investors

While you, your grandmother and your best friend Scooter have all put money into your startup, chances are none of you are accredited investors.

In order to be accredited, you need to learn how to deal with securities that are not registered with financial authorities. You'll have to satisfy one of several requirements, including income, net worth, level of assets and professional/governance experience. Being accredited has some serious requirements.

Becoming accredited might not be on your radar. But to take your startup to the next level, you're going to need a bunch of these folks to write you checks.

If you've already raised First Money, you're about to enter the big leagues — Angel, Seed and Venture Capital. These folks are the big risk takers and they're tough as nails. Plus, they're probably 5x more knowledgable about your business than you are.

To land your first big fish, you'll present 10-20 slides in front of 100 people at a networking event, after which a couple of socially awkward robots will approach you and say that they want to invest in you and your company.

These wealthy gems will be the most important people you've met to date.

You have one shot with an investor. Take advantage of it by presenting riveting opportunities that are both obvious and revenue-generating. By "obvious," I mean products and models that they can quickly understand.

Keep in mind that investors are usually intelligent, but some of them might have more money than brains. Too much money can inflate a person's confidence and self-perception. Suffice to say, never overvalue an investors input, but take all input into consideration.

After you've convinced Family, Friends & Sweethearts to invest in your startup, here are the next conquests:

1. Angel Investors (Micro VCs)

The word angel fills my heart with warm-fuzzy feelings because I imagine ethereal beings protecting me. Truth be told, Angels often do more due diligence than venture capital firms (VC Firms). Angels might also syndicate their deals in the millions of dollars, which means that they're not really Angels, they're more like bankers. Their gentle, hometown masks are a front. These cash-jockeys are intense and powerful.

Angels are often accredited investors who tend to invest between $10K and $25K per venture. Once you land Angel investors, you must do everything necessary to grow your relationships with them. This includes babysitting their overprivileged kids, washing their monogramed cars, and inviting them to your hipster parties. It really helps if you get them high.

These folks are the first business people to validate your happy, hippie startup train. They'll introduce you to deep pockets. Without their braintrusts, you're just one more dipshit in a sea of douchebags looking for funding for a pie-in-the-sky model, that we all know is full of gaping holes, epic lies and fairy dust.

2. Seed Capital (Micro VCs)

Staffed by full-time investors and professionals, Micros manage funds between $10MM and $25MM. Some are hyper-focused on niches, but it seems that many of these groups spend across several industries and categories. As a collective, they invest in the range of $100K to $2.5MM.

Micro VCs often fall between being experienced and not-so-experienced. They're akin to the teenager who got laid once but who tells all of his friends that he gets laid all the time. These guys are a little cocky and sometimes a little clueless. As they do due-diligence on you, you'll want to do the same on them.

3. Venture Capital

These are the "big boys." Companies like Greylock, Sequoia, Kleiner and Spark Capital are called venture capital firms. They have anywhere from $40MM to $100MM ready to invest in startups and other businesses that are further down the line.

Their investments come in the form of Series A, B, C, etc., known as "rounds." While these folks might also come in at the Angel or Seed level, it doesn't define them as such because of the size of their fund, how tight their sphincters are, and how long they'll most likely stay in your game.

Venture Capital monkeys have a wide range of personalities. Some are kind, open and willing to listen. This denotes their graciousness and intelligence. Others will lecture you for 17 minutes on how much they know about your industry before giving you three minutes to deliver your entire presentation. Feel free to interrupt these motormouths. It's your meeting too!

These life-cycle investors might invest every time your company needs money, all the way up to the IPO (Initial Public Offering) when you go public, and are traded on the NY Stock Exchange (NYSE), The American Stock Exchange (AMEX) or other exchanges around the world.

Having meetings with these groups is super-exciting. There's usually four to eight people in the room, each one of them hyper-focused on vetting the living shit out of you, your Big Idea and your presentation.

Not one person in that room is looking to be your friend. They don't give a crap about you. These are man-eating sharks. Their sole purpose is to become intimately aware of every facet of your Big Idea. They see thousands of presentations every year. Get to the point, assume that they know your business better than you, and be ready for pushback on everything. In short, be prepared.

Venture capital firms might ponder how your idea might benefit one of their already-existing companies, possibly for a quick purchase. They might also consider how your idea would be a great pivot for one of their companies, leaving you in the lurch. Technically, this isn't stealing since you haven't hit the market yet. At least that's how they'll look at it.

Be prepared for some dark forces to be in that room. To them, this is not an exciting moment to celebrate a dream. It's an opportunity for them to look good to their firm and to advance their personal wealth. If your deal has some mojo, expect these hungry wolves to bite.

4. Grants

There are hundreds of grants available to entrepreneurs and small businesses in a variety of categories. This is free money that does not affect your percentage of ownership. You'll want to hire a professional grant writer to help you out because it can be difficult to land a grant.

If you don't have a product in the market just yet, you might consider an approach that includes the pursuit of Angels, Seed Capital and Grants. This will give you traction in three categories and their respective communities.

Raising money is a full-time job. The most important things for you to remember are to be prepared and to be grateful when somebody gives you enough money to fund your dream.

Accredited investors are usually grumpy naysayers who've seen 80% of your presentation at least 200 times.

Be prepared, be honest, lose the hype, and memorize your business model as if it's your last conscious action on planet Earth.

FunFacts

Defensive CEOs quickly repel investors and they rarely raise money. *

Solo founders take 3.6x longer to reach the point at which their companies scale and no longer need venture capital. *

When you blush, the lining of your stomach blushes too. *

Common mistakes in failed startups include: *

1) Going into business for the wrong reasons.

2) Taking advice from family or friends.

3) Lack of market awareness.

4) Lack of clear focus.

(*) Startupgenome.com, Fast Company, TechWorld.com, PaulGraham.com, Distractify.com

26 Board of Directors

Your board should be comprised of the most powerful people in your network. The most awe-inspiring board members are difficult to find and even tougher to lock down. They're elusive, like magical wood nymphs.

Some board members are promised seats at the table upon investment, while others are strategic non-investors with the sole mission of helping you to advance your business. Regardless, most board members are just friendly blowhards.

When you get some of these over-pedigreed blabber-mouths in the same room, there can be so much hot air that you might feel like you're in a wind tunnel. When they're not speaking, they're usually sucking on a pen. Oral fixations are their favorite past times.

Many of these guys picked up their bad habits from their racist, emotionally challenged fathers, while growing up on exclusive golf courses where everybody wore the same pants. After 9 holes, you might see one of them in the locker room, snapping one off to his own image.

The moment that these moth-eaten artifacts join your board, they can immediately forget how to be helpful.

Instead, they behave like monkeys competing for bananas. You have to push them into being useful.

How do you avoid all the monkeys and land the most stirring board members? First, get rid of all the bananas. Next, seek out people that you admire, who have qualities that you love. Tell them how much you respect them and want to be more like them. Invite them to coffee or lunch. Give them a career-related gift or find the perfect gift for their kids. Quality people never forget generous acts.

When you finally meet these iconic egos, grill them like you're a New York Times journalist who just landed an interview with the aliens secretly running our government.

Dig deep and get to know them personally. Learn how they think and how they work. Inquire about their cultures, backgrounds and biggest decisions. Ask about their mistakes, challenges and most enduring successes. Encourage them to tell you a secret or two.

When you piece together the puzzle, you might find that they're the perfect fit. You also might find that they are more like 2D cartoons than multi-dimensional human beings.

Some big-shot executives don't give a hoot about startups, they just want deal flow. They might expect that your project will either make them more relevant or put them into more lucrative circles.

Meet potential board members in networking groups. Just remember that some of the board-sluts who hang out in these groups are only concerned about title, money and position. They might be cordial at cocktail parties, but they'll stab your back for profit.

Your board members are not your friends, but let them earn your trust over time. Ideally, they should be hard-working rock stars who regularly prove themselves by delivering value.

Consider board members who have unique cultures and backgrounds. Seek people who are passionate, open-minded and connected to strong networks.

You might consider making room for board members who've recently been through hell and back. They might not appear to be in good shape physically, mentally or emotionally, but you can learn a lot from people who've risen from the dead.

Be selfish when building your board. Don't invite them to join because you feel sorry for them, or because you want to give them a leg up. Bring on board members to serve your startup, ones who have already proven themselves in the world.

Make sure you need your board members WAY MORE than they need you.

Do not, for any reason, put family members on your board. And forget about your alcoholic college pals. You already know these people. You've already bonded with them, and absorbed their intel and styles. You need fresh minds and meat.

One reason startups fail is because their CEOs prefer taking advice from their drunk friends, quasi-family advisors and no-experience, sideline cheerleaders rather than seasoned professionals.

It's as if these founders can't survive unless they're surrounded by weak-minded savants and intellectually bankrupt fluffers who've seen them naked. This invites dangerous levels of comfort and delusions of grandeur. It's a sure-fire path to self-inflicted disaster.

Your board should be 100X smarter and 200X more connected than you. If your board is filled with people who are unable to outpace and out-think you, that's not a board of directors, it's a cocktail party.

Your board should make you uncomfortable by putting carrots in front of you to help the business grow. If they're not kicking your ass, they're asleep. Toss 'em.

Some startup CEOs fire board members when they perceive them to be too tough or unreasonable. Don't be a wimp. If your board is being tough on you, it's probably because you fucked up. You either scaled too soon, overspent or got caught doing blow at your neighbor's kid's birthday party. Own it.

At every juncture, take the licks you deserve, especially when they come from your board. It's a great way to learn. Don't ever blame your board for challenging your fantasies. If you're looking to get your ass kissed, don't launch a startup, become a priest.

Fill your board and advisory with respectable, hard-working winners who have integrity.

Remember, you're not a charity.

27 Accelerators & Incubators

Accelerators and incubators are similar creatures. They counsel startups on how to get to the next level, they offer networks of mentors and advisors and they help founders turn their warm-fuzzy dreams into actionable plans.

While accelerators focus on prepping startups for investors, incubators provide startups education and stability, and help founders build their teams. Incubators are more like pre-school, while accelerators are like MBAs, but without all that sleepy 1950s curriculum.

Accelerators and some incubators give startups small seed investments ($20K to $250K) plus access to hundreds of advisors (who might also be investors). In exchange, startups give these organizations small percentages of their companies (3% to 20%). They state the deal on the applications when you apply. If you get in, it's awesome.

At the conclusion of accelerator programs, startups pitch to rooms full of investors and journalists. This is "Demonstration Day," the most exciting day of your life. Seriously, it's better than sex on a roller coaster.

Incubators, on the other hand, often focus on super-young companies. The founders might be college students or super-newbies with menial day-jobs, for example, staring out windows.

Some incubators are funded by venture capital firms, government agencies, or divisions of corporations. In some cases, incubators require that your startup be in specific categories of business, such as healthcare, robotics, manufacturing or naked dance parties.

Incubators might require travel to their headquarters, where an education is provided, or where you might live for a while so that you can gain access to everything that they have to offer. Accelerators require travel too, but often for shorter periods of time.

At accelerators and incubators alike, you'll enjoy co-working environments where, if you're broke, you can live off of their snacks and sleep in one of their closets. Be sure to bring a pillow.

In both scenarios, you'll participate in one-week to six-month social and educational experiences, where you'll build out your product, perfect your presentation and show your stuff to investors, some of whom might pony up on the spot. Other investors will "date" your startup for months, but never let you get to second base.

Rather than list every accelerator and incubator here, check out the whole shebang at <u>F6S.com</u>. This is the Mother of All Accelerator Social Networks. It's a beast that lists all of them.

Equally helpful is <u>angel.co</u>, where you can network with fellow founders, meet investors and create profiles that make you sound like you deserve a Nobel Peace Prize.

The challenge with incubators is that they sometimes fail to nudge startups out of the gate. The problem with accelerators is that they're built to pump you up and give you a happy ending, even though happy endings are rare, unless you're in Thailand. To be successful in either, it comes down to hard work and networking.

A few startups will raise angel funding on Demonstration Days, but most will receive $10 gift cards so that they can buy socks. Either way, you'll learn whether or not your Big Idea is worthy of a three year commitment and a life-long nervous tick.

Some of the guys who lead accelerators are full of goodness and integrity. They live to serve others. It's super exciting to be around these people. They will follow you around like puppy dogs seeing how they can help you. They're saintly and brilliant.

You might also meet a few egomaniacs who see you as a marketable piece of meat. This doesn't mean that they're bad people, it just means that they're wolves and you're Little Red Riding Hood. Be alert.

When applying to accelerators, look for the ones with 20% of the curriculum aimed at customer discovery. Without a customer dialogues, the only things you'll be bringing home are gift cards and new socks.

Some accelerators and incubators are life-changing. They introduce you to hundreds of people and they help you take major steps forward. Some are attaboy clubs that send participants down egoistic rabbit holes. Vet them with intensity. Remember, this is YOUR LIFE!

Most startup folks will go out of their way to help you, but some of these people are opportunists hoping to use you as a disposable diaper.

I was once on a panel for a startup competition. Six startup founders presented their companies. There was only one clear winner of this contest, a new startup, full of obsessive, aligned, hard-working twenty-somethings. They were the underdogs, broke, brilliant, hungry, eager and they had developed a great MVP.

Unfortunately, my banker panel-mates were pushing for a different winner, a startup that had just raised over $2.5MM, and in which two of the judges had already invested. I fought these moneybags to agree to a tie between the real winner and the tainted, funded pony. Fuck the tainted pony!

Tiny prizes can fund important aspects in feisty young startups, like food for their starving CEOs. Meanwhile, when tiny cash prizes are given to multi-million dollar "startups," they might buy caviar and lap dances.

Some investors will tell you that startups can have 30 shareholders and $10MM in venture capital, but that's a lie. This is how greedy investors garner press for their well-funded businesses, thus increasing their wealth. It's misleading. If your investment has a few million in the bank, it's unethical to call it a startup. Get your hands out of the kiddie pool, you putz!

While there will always be soulless, greedy putzel-fucks in the world, most accelerators, incubators and contests are wonderful funnels that feed venture capital to young, scrappy startups.

Now that you've got the perfect product, 100 completed customer interviews, four patents in process, two mentors, eight advisors, a solid board of directors, and you've moved into that new co-working space, changed your diet and started looking for the best accelerators, you are well on your way to being wealthy beyond your dreams, having a live-in physician, and simultaneously living on the beach, in the mountains and inside your custom, nuclear-powered, submersible mansion. Kudos!

Evaluate every aspect of the accelerators and incubators that you like. Look at their boards, leaders and managers. Check out their processes and procedures. Most importantly, don't put up with any crap from the bad ones.

Remember, this is YOUR LIFE!

28 For Investors Only

Every entrepreneur is scared shitless about meeting you. They've looked you up online, memorized your profile, researched your hobbies, Facebooked your kids, and every morning they recite your name 1008 times, like a mantra. Entrepreneurs are obsessed with investors. They'll travel a thousand miles on a scooter just to lick your windshield.

To them, you are Mommy, Daddy, best friend, girlfriend, boyfriend and the bank all rolled into one massive, multiplex projection. You are The Eternal Icon of Benevolence. They can't help it. Entrepreneurs are just wired that way. I know, it's fucked up.

Every entrepreneur that you'll meet will have been practicing their presentation for 84 hours straight. They haven't slept since the inception of their idea two years ago, and they ran out of money last week. Their most recent meal was three nights ago, at a bakery that gave them free stale bread.

Most entrepreneurs are so consumed with raising money that they are moments away from being carted off to the nut-house. They're living off free samples at the Dollar Store and cleaning toilets with toothbrushes just to get by. Seriously, keep a healthy distance.

I know you. We've invested together and we've been on panels together. I love you, but let's face it, you can be a putz when meeting entrepreneurs. Even if you're the biggest butthole in the universe, please pretend to be a human being when dealing with startups. You can do it!

Examples of two solid human beings in the venture capital world are Peter Adams and Dave Harris at Colorado's Rockies Venture Club.

I've met lots of the big players around the world, but these guys are The Gods of Graciousness, the anti-humble-braggers, the folks anyone would enjoy doing business with. They are so discreet and accommodating that you quickly forget why you visited their MBA man-cave in the first place.

When you first shake Peter's and Dave's hands, and see the warmth in their eyes, you'll want to grab your blankie and cuddle with them. These guys ooze charisma. If that's a bit much for you, then you'll at least want to grab a beer with them, shoot the shit and play darts. They're that cool.

The guys at Rockies Venture Club are smart enough to know that every presentation that they see is an opportunity to learn something. If that weren't enough, they're also straight-forward and encouraging human beings. Outstanding, right?

Brad Feld is the same way. He's always looking for ways to enlighten the startup community through blogs, books and more. This type of benevolence is rare in this world and it should be celebrated.

Kindness is beneficial for everybody, unless you're dealing with a dishonest sociopath. In that case, just smack the person around until he leaves your network.

Whether you're a crusty old investor or a nouveau-riche tech-twat, please consider these ideas:

1. *Be friendly to the entrepreneurs you meet.*

2. *If they're presenting to you, help them relax. Ask their names and ask them how they're doing.*

3. *Tell them that you're looking forward to hearing more about their startup and their Big Ideas. Before they get started, give them a compliment.*

4. *Keep in mind that after presentations, founders are nervous, raw, unstable, sensitive, nauseated, and potentially freaked out and in need of medication. They're tiny birds who just fell 200 feet from their nests. They might even have a concussion.*

5. *If you are unhappy with their premise, or if their proposition is outside your usual category, ask a few questions anyway. This will give the entrepreneurs a will to live. They might even sleep that night.*

6. *If you're interested in the premise, get to know the team. Take them out to dinner. Ask them a lot of personal questions, not to make them feel good, but to find out what's under the hood. Evaluate their personalities and look for signs of psychoses. Seriously, some of these mutherf*ckers are nuts.*

7. *Dive into the mistakes that these entrepreneurs made. Source the holes in their thinking and attitudes. Make*

sure that they're open to feedback so that you can guide them along the way.

8. *Before signing on the dotted line, ask for access to the CEO's budget and model. Dig into their assumptions. Question their beliefs. Ask about their ramp-up plans.*

9. *Always ask to speak to all current and former board members and investors. Put this in your contract. Some CEOs don't want you to know their dirty secrets or how they screwed everybody during the previous rounds. This happens all the time. Dig deep, play the sleuth and take notes. Be ready to pounce if they've misled you.*

10. *If you don't know enough about a startup's industry, do extensive research or skip this one. I always say, "Be in the know or don't go."*

After their presentations, some entrepreneurs refuse to hear critical feedback. Even after hearing the most harmonious of notes, they might curse, punch a wall or burst into tears. They might even become defensive when you say, "Nice job!"

Truth be told, many entrepreneurs are not humble enough to run startups. These insecure chuckleheads may have become too convinced of their own brilliance, and are only able to hear feedback that's tucked betwixt an ass-kissing and a hand-job. They might tell you that they're listening, all the while, they'll resent you for your critique. It's actually legal to smack these founders in the head and draw blood.

In the early stages of an investment, find out if your entrepreneurs are taking your advice. Some of these whack-a-moles will fool you by yessing you to death for months. You might not find out until a year later that they never intended to listen to your feedback, EVER. Meanwhile, they're driving the company to its untimely death, like Thelma and Louise.

Many founders are allergic to business acumen. They think that they've got it all figured out.

There are solid, accountable people in the startup community, but there are also bogus posers. One of my favorite dipsticks is Dicky Disingenuous. Dicky saunters around startup events pretending to be the penultimate investor, the Jesus H. Buddha of Funding. He's got a happy-dippy, priestly face, but then he opens his mouth. He is so inappropriately critical of vulnerable startups, he'll lecture them without ever being asked for his feedback. Don't be this guy.

My biggest hope for all of you is to have empathy as often as possible. If a founder asks you for help, it's okay to be tough, even grumpy, just try to balance your attitude with a little kindness. Being critical is helpful. Being a jack-off is not — well, unless the founder you're dealing with is duplicitous, manipulative or a downright liar. We've all met these types of entrepreneurs. They're exhausting!

Some entrepreneurs will never understand honesty or gratitude, which I discuss in other chapters. They'll hound you and coerce you into hating them. It's okay to bounce the windbags who have zero respect for you.

If your heart is truly committed to innovation, then mentor a startup. Find the scrappiest, most humble, most clueless team and wrap your arms around them. Give them encouragement and advise them on how to take their Big Ideas to the next level. This is what Fred Silverman did for me and it changed my life.

I know I've been tough on you investors in this chapter, but let's face it, you have a big pretty house, a fascinating bilingual mistress and a 33% stake in a private jet. Your slippers are made of Kobe cow leather and they're wrapped in virgin Venezuelan bunny fur.

My point is this: While basking in the glory of the top 2%, remember that you're also a human being. Preserve your openness, your loving nature and your ability to encourage and empathize with others. Stay human. It's your most beautiful, most powerful quality.

Continually nurture your heart and stay connected to it. It's the only thing that you have any control over.

When investors are kind to entrepreneurs, these passionate, inventive souls are happier and more balanced as they pursue and build their dreams.

Be humane so that you'll inspire new founders to respect and love themselves.

 Legal Bullshit

If you're reading this book and you're a lawyer who wants to be more entrepreneurial, you're taking a huge step toward becoming a human being. Congratulations!

However, if you're thin-skinned about being a lawyer, and if anti-lawyer sentiments crawl up your skirt and give you hives, you might want to skip to the next chapter. There might be some carnage here.

While lawyers might be sexy when getting all lawyer-y, there's nothing sexy about wasting your money on services that you can do for yourself. No matter what most lawyers say, they don't have your best interests at heart and they won't provide quality services at fair prices. Mostly, they molest you — with invoices.

If your cute little startup is penniless, incorporate the company yourselves and write your own founder agreements. Hiring a lawyer at this stage would be like buying a Porsche so that you can deliver pizzas. Kinda silly, right? Especially when you can pick up a lifetime of legal education online.

Your best tactic is to set up meetings with six to ten law firms in your area. Include individuals, two-person firms, mid-size firms and multinational law firms. For each of these meetings, dress like it's a Presidential Ball and act as if you'd like to hire them to do a billion dollars of legal work — TOMORROW!

Get them excited about the fact that you're the bastard child from a marriage between a Koch and a Rockefeller, and that you chair a global trust with $50B in assets in 30 countries, all of which need legal representation — YESTERDAY!

For fun, casually mention that you own a manufacturing plant on a tropical island that's staffed with an indigenous tribe of miniature people, who provide free labor in exchange for berries.

To derive the most benefit from these meetings, ask these blabbermouths every question you can think of, take notes and be sure to overstay your welcome. Don't leave until they drag you out in restraints.

Be prepared to be un-invited at the 45 minute mark. If they let you stay longer than that, they might want sex. If you find this appealing, act quickly, because lawyers lie and change their minds a lot.

Schedule second and third meetings with the lawyers who were the most forthcoming with information. Even if you respect one of these lawyers, at no time should you hire her. Just buy her chocolates as a thank you.

ALL lawyers are ambulance chasers, each in their own unique way. Every lawyer hides behind a mask, especially when he's shaking you down for cash.

Don't be impressed with firm handshakes or how they repeat your name multiple times during the meeting.

Equally manipulating is when the truly flashy ones bring 25 partners into the 8-person conference room so that you can experience a gaggle of ass-kissers, all speaking from the same contrived, soulless lexicon. They might even serve you a box lunch.

Some lawyers are vampires hoping to suck the life out of you. At the tail of your meetings, notice how some of them look at your neck. That's because they're hunting for the best vein.

It always starts with "We'll do everything for you, and we'll keep it simple and inexpensive!" It's never simple or inexpensive. They'll tally up everything. They'll even charge you extra if your contract uses too many fonts.

If you must have a lawyer, set boundaries with him. In your engagement letter, include a clause that says, "Before providing any ridiculous billable service, I must approve it via email or carrier pigeon." Otherwise, he'll find lots of ways to get approvals for things that a monkey could do. By the way, I love monkeys.

When Fred Silverman and I worked together, we hired the Los Angeles law firm of Cheaters, Scammers & Hypocrites to set up our venture. I believe their favorite movie was *Swindler's List*, a lovely film about a group of hero-brokers who cheated poor families for profit.

When I first called these con artists with a question, they put four lawyers on the phone to answer it. I think the question was, "Hi." I found out later that we were billed for every second with each of the four lawyers. Hell, the fucking secretary could have answered our questions. She was brilliant.

One of these evil-lawyers said to me, "Since Fred is your ATM, what does it matter how much you spend on legal?" My response was simple, "Listen scumbag, don't call my investor and partner an ATM. He's a man who is managing his finances just like the rest of us. HIS pain is MY pain, you greedy clipped-dick douche."

If you need an operating agreement or a term sheet, just ask another startup founder to give you their paperwork, then just fill in the blanks. As a thank you, give them a gift card from Whole Foods. When you've got it all filled out, only then would I hire a friend-lawyer to make sure the document is "good enough for now."

When you give a lawyer a document that they didn't write, EVERY ONE OF THEM will tell you that it needs to be rewritten. It could have been drafted by the firm of Jesus, Mozart and Einstein, but they'll bounce it back to you saying it's inadequate.

Do you know why they don't like to edit other lawyers' contracts — because they don't like to read! They don't want to read or edit anything. Their brains are only geared for accepting direct deposits.

And here's what you'll be billed for: The number of hours that they think the document is worth, had they written it from scratch, which they did only once, and will continue to sell off as custom legal work until they're 90. All they do is copy, paste, fill in blanks and sell copies of documents thousands of times.

You'll only need a lawyer if you're taking on investors, getting sued, defending your intellectual property or if you've been caught masturbating in church.

You can create your own documents for incorporation, patents, copyrights and trademarks online. It'll take a few weeks to learn how to do everything, but it'll be worth it. This will save you thousands of dollars.

Only as your company's cash flow increases, should you hire a lawyer to clean up the negligible mistakes you might have made along the way. If you hire them too soon, lawyers can bankrupt you and abort your cute little startup.

Don't even look at your lawyer. Seriously. They know that you're thinking about them right now. Stop it! Otherwise, you'll wake up to a pile of invoices.

If you're a lawyer, I dare you to be transparent with your clients about actual time spent. You'll become known as the only startup-saving lawyer in the world.

You know what transparency is? It's open, honest billing related to the work you do. Lawyers are never transparent. I can just hear the lawyers who are reading this right now, telling me to go fuck myself. Well, right back atcha you fucking skunk. Seriously, put away those deposit slips and pickup the mirror — to your soul.

Law firms are similar to traveling carnivals, where each lawyer is commissioned to pull customers into the big tent, and tell stories that showcase their firm as a phenomenon, bearded ladies and all. It's a show.

There will be times when you'll need a lawyer. Take your time to find an honest one and don't let them invoice you every time they take a shit. I'm lucky to know a few good ones should you need a referral.

The same can be said for some bankers. These clandestine cubical-monkeys will promise you the world, as if they've ever seen it, but they too often behave like soulless robots.

Bankers will say, "We love the community and all the beautiful small businesses!" But they don't lend to small businesses. They lend to companies that do not need money. And they don't care about people. Every decision they make is derived from an algorithm, not someone's heart. Don't buy their bullshit.

Some bankers and lawyers will continually verbal-vomit their unsolicited, irrelevant advice to you and then try to relate it to their overhyped services, but they don't walk in your shoes. They wouldn't be caught dead in your shoes. They don't even call them shoes. Every pricey thing on their bodies is a brand. "Oh, my Manolos got poo on them. Darn it!"

Do your own legal work and find a credit union. Take your power back and put it to work. You've got a brain. Use it.

Lawyers are money-hungry miscreants hoping to make millions with their ability to use "cut and paste." Upon meeting you, lawyers secretly think, "Hello little ATM!

SIGN HERE _____."

Checklist #5

Bang out in under an hour:

☐ Complete a super-awesome version of your executive summary. Be in love with it.

☐ Using an online template, create a final draft of your Cap Table.

☐ Write a list of the investors who you know and a list of the investors you would like to meet.

Requires additional time and effort:

☐ Continue perfecting your executive summary, business model & canvas, and presentation.

☐ Revisit your Operating Agreements and do the necessary research to perfect them.

☐ Revisit your Operating Plans and do the necessary research to perfect them.

☐ Perfect your Cap Table one last time.

☐ Reach out to your favorite investor and schedule your first presentation with them.

☐ Apply to five incubators or accelerators.

☐ Take a few days and go on a road trip, participate in an adventure or get in a little trouble. Just don't get caught or arrested.

☐ Within the week, select and read a book from the Author's Favorite Books.

☐ Do something silly or romantic with your lover, partner or closest friends.

Marketing

Marketing is a snake that continually changes its skin. It's wildly unpredictable. Yet without marketing, your predictive robot accessory will join the millions of other gadgets and apps now resting in unmarked graves.

The biggest problem is that startups rarely have the money to fund impactful marketing campaigns, yet many of them will drop 50% of the $50K they have in the bank on marketing. These folks always end up screwing themselves and their companies. Sit tight on marketing until you have the right level of cash.

Marketing is so horribly expensive, complex and subjective that spending money on marketing is equal to gambling. For example, your chance of success is akin to playing Roulette at a casino. Besides gobs of cash, successful campaigns require time to evolve.

Many marketing plans are more egoistic than intelligent because most marketers pretend that they have all the answers, when in most cases, they're either guessing or lying. Sadly, marketing is rarely a noble, thoughtful endeavor. Until your marketers prove themselves, think of them as slap-happy clowns.

Let's get a few definitions out of the way.

Social media marketing (SMM) consists of using web services and social networks to display ads and hyper-focused content to specific groups. You hire marketing teams to make engaging content that connects with your customers. The hope is to promote the content so as to produce a blinding mad rush to your store. Yeah, good luck with that.

Traditional marketing is television ads, print ads in magazines and newspapers, newsletters, billboards and flyers. Strangely, this is still effective. Be aware that many ad sales people live in 1957, and aren't fully aware of how to negotiate a deal or retain customers.

Email marketing delivers the biggest bang for the buck. The idea being that when you send out five million emails, it will form an insanely addictive religion around your product, causing people to jump out of buildings if they don't get one.

Be aware that slick email sales thieves will try to sell you 1000 email addresses for $25K. It's a scam. Research the cheapest and most highly specified email lists, then do the deal with the lowest bid. Better yet, build your own lists organically through your website. With lists in hand, find the best tools to monitor the success of your outreach.

Public relations means hiring caffeine-addicted twenty somethings to write riveting articles that will magically appear in every household in 37 countries. While these articles will enhance your self-esteem, they often amount to a big pile of, "I can't stop yawning".

Phone banks are groups of people, in a variety of countries, who aggressively call lists of your potential customers and try to convince them that they speak english, and that without your product they might die.

You can also attend startup events and run up and down the aisles screaming, "WE FIGURED IT OUT! WE SOLVED IT! VISIT MY BOOTH! IT WILL CHANGE THE LIVES OF YOUR CHILDREN'S CHILDREN!" Strangely, this also works fairly well.

The other tool is lying. This is what most companies do. They just lie their asses off. Why? It's legal.

Consider evil soft drink executives who sell sugar, diabetes and cancer to children and families. While their slogans say, "We love you!", they actually mean, "We make billions of dollars buying local water supplies and selling it back to you as cancerous sludge!"

What to do?! Do you lie like these assholes, do you email, do you hire marketing teams, or do you just hope for articles to be written about you so that you can become the ambassador of fill-in-the-blank.

There are a few things that you can do.

1. Crawl into a hole and say, "Fuck marketing!"

2. Do a combination of traditional advertising, social media marketing, email marketing, PR, phone banks, lying, guerrilla theater, oral sex and flash mobs.

3. Hire a fractional CMO and/or a part-time Market Analyst to build out a massive strategy. This might be overkill at the start, but it'll give you a killer education about what is ahead of you.

You can use Facebook, Twitter, Google ads and others to bang out a few ads and test them on a few groups. You can then use analytics tools to monitor your success. Slowly build on this. Do not mortgage your house or children just yet. Upon traction, you can upgrade your text and image ads to video, and you can customize your content so that it better educates and enthuses your potential customers.

All that said, you're still gambling. If you're just starting out, put together one big email list, comprised of address from all of your friends and all of the friends of your founders and employees. Send an email to all of them that says, "Hi, I love you, please try our product."

As your revenue increases, allocate more money to marketing. Keep in mind that product development and real-world customer relationships are far more valuable than any complex marketing strategy or campaign.

Be careful. Some marketers are akin to organ harvesters. They get rich and you can't breathe.

Marketing should be studied carefully. A solid book on the subject is, _Marketing Strategy: Based on First Principles and Data Analytics_, by Robert W. Palmatier and Shrihari Sridhar. It's a punch in the face. Enjoy it!

Marketing is like a drug-addicted teenager. Don't give it a dime until you understand what that money is funding. Follow the trends. They're constantly changing.

Checklist #6

Bang out in under an hour:

☐ Read 5 articles about the current and future trends of marketing.

☐ Make a list of the top 25 websites that your customers most likely regularly enjoy.

☐ Make a list of a few of the marketing strategies that your competitors are using.

☐ Email ten online newspaper/magazine reporters. Ask them if they'd consider writing articles about your company's products.

☐ Research 5 upcoming marketing education events and commit to attending one of them.

Requires additional time and effort:

☐ Ask your network for referrals to qualified CMOs, Social Media Managers and Marketing Directors. Take a few of them out for coffee and ask them questions until they beg to leave.

☐ Ask your network for introductions to Market Analysts. Take a few of these geniuses out to lunch. Beg them to help you in exchange for one percentage point in your company. These magic gnomes are usually the primary transformers of businesses.

☐ Read one top-notch marketing book this week, then call a few of your new marketing contacts to discuss it with them over the phone.

☐ Get a massage and buy yourself a gift.

31 Personhood

My career has been a gripping, multi-faceted thrill ride. Just ask anyone. I spent years as a computer system's analyst, toured the world twice as a professional and corporate comedian, had TV and radio shows, lived in several countries and have had adventures most people only dream about. I'm a very lucky person.

I've lived at ashrams in India, meditated at countless temples in China, studied with Native American elders and I've done several long stints in the wilderness.

I've written books on personal development and I've taught, facilitated or participated in over 1000 workshops and rituals related to spiritual growth.

With that said, you might find this chapter just a teensy bit off topic — but it's not. There is nothing more important than improving upon how you perceive yourself and the world that you live in. It's also crucial to understand your connection with the universe and how it perceives you.

I believe that it's impossible to arrive at excellence in our businesses without seeking excellence within ourselves. The more that we know about ourselves and the more we love ourselves, the better chances we have at success.

Our challenge is that most of us are part angel, part devil. We'll joyfully hurt others, then beat ourselves up as penance. We may have become so lost in dark doorways so long ago, that we no longer remember the pathways home. We forget how to give and we forget how to receive. Hiding from the secrets nestled in our past, we hold ourselves accountable for every transgression. We are complex creatures to say the least.

We've all made huge mistakes and we have all come to regret them. Each of us are also subject to the misgivings of others, which we must forgive without regret. If we don't move on, we take it with us.

The biggest challenge is remaining honest during the process of starting a business. Delusion isn't just an idea, it's an addiction. It arises out of insecurity and fear. It takes a special kind of person to dissolve it.

Here are a few ideas that I believe will help you to advance your personal excellence and move into the present moment without fear. These things will also improve your business. I'm sure of it.

Your Body

Although I joke a lot about it, we do not need any intoxicating substances to make our lives better. If you struggle with depression or swinging emotions, realize that everything you put into your body affects you.

Alcohol and pot can be fun, but they are intense sedatives that require titration. Every drink and toke produces a chemical reaction that requires a balancing, even if the substance is perceived to be medicinal. Sugar is no different. When it comes to how our bodies experience it, sugar is akin to cocaine.

Honor yourself. Be careful with your body. Everything you put into it goes into your heart and mind, and eventually your family and business.

Alignment vs. Enrollment

Finding alignment with others is less stressful and requires less energy than trying to enroll them. It also produces greater results. The same can be said about our relationships with ourselves. Seek to understand other people's ideas and attributes. Do not judge them.

When we seek ways to understand another's beliefs, we find far more similarities than differences.

Lovingly Allow Mistakes, But Don't Be A Doormat

We should allow for mistakes from every person we engage. Some people might seek to challenge or undo our goodness. They might use us, or refuse to appreciate us.

These people have a hard time giving freely of themselves, because they're scared to be open and generous. Move quickly from these types of individuals. Snap off the branch and be free.

Laugh At Yourself

Laughing at ourselves helps the universe to see our vulnerabilities and humility. Laughter opens up the flood gates to goodness. When we're vulnerable, the universe meets us halfway and co-creates our dreams with us. Self-deprecation keeps us humble. Let's laugh heartily and free ourselves from what we are not.

Express Your Emotions

It's healthy to cry when we feel hurt. When you're angry, find a healthy, non-violent way to express it. If you feel trapped or stifled, pound the Earth! Focus on the imagery and thoughts that feel charged or unresolved. Explore every tangent of your emotional tree. With every tear, we achieve an understanding. Without emotion, there is no wisdom.

Forensic Forgiveness

Unwind ancient anger, sadness and regret through deep forgiveness. Release these trapped energies through emotions. You'll have more vibrancy and you'll naturally be more attractive. Dig deep and let it go.

Thoughts Are Everything

Reality creates itself from our thoughts. With every thought we have, we create ourselves and our worlds. Nourish only the thoughts that bring your heart, talents and happiness into focus. Think fondly of those you love and all of those with whom you engage. Our thoughts are the creators of our happiness and the gatekeepers to our future selves.

Be Authentic

Today's corporate lingo is vaporware. It's politically correct, controlled, contrived and coachy. Be authentic and speak your truth. Let it out! Swear like a truck driver if that's your style!

Letting Go

Choose and change relationships in favor of your happiness. Your contract is not with individuals. It is with the universe. Remember too that it's okay to completely let someone or something go without an explanation. The resulting peacefulness is a gift that you give to yourself, and the universe smiles upon it.

Make Joyful Decisions

Give yourself a precious gift right now: Make a bold, empowering, joyful decision. Induce a new beginning for yourself, one that promises your heart an unbridled freedom of expression. Do it right now.

In The World

Appreciate the people that you meet. Look for positive things to say to them. If they have offended you, let them know (or don't) and then move on. If you are continually giving positive feedback to others, you will receive an equal measure of positivity in return. In all things, choose relationships, businesses and actions that serve your clarity and joy.

If you're not improving yourself, you're not in the business of success.

the only person you can change

the only **person** you can affect

the only person **you** can control

the only person you **can** push

the only person you can rage against

the only person who can inspire your
transformation

the only person that you ever interact with

is

FunFacts

60% of founders have at least one child, who will eventually be in therapy because her mommy and daddy lost their minds running startups. *

Self-employed people are able to create multiple revenue streams, while those who are regularly employed usually have only one revenue stream. *

When in love, the human brain releases the same neurotransmitters and hormones that are released by amphetamines. This leads to increased heart rate, loss of appetite, nervousness and has the potential to make you behave like an idiot. *

As a startup founder, you'll build alliances with people that you will never like or trust. *

(*) Kauffman Foundation, Inc.com, PaulGraham.com, Distractify.com

32 Management Principles

1. Be grateful for every person at your table. Fight to keep them there.

2. Keep your word and help others to do the same.

3. Take advice from people who are smarter than you or who know your industry better than you.

4. If you feel that you're an island, you probably are.

5. Regularly give back to your community.

6. Get to the point. Don't waste other people's time.

7. Get to know your employees so that you better understand their value and ways to successfully encourage and motivate them.

8. Find ways to love your work. This is mandatory.

9. If you feel the need to cry, go for it. It's not 1950. Let it all out.

10. Establish a diverse working environment. Include women and lots of unique backgrounds and cultures.

11. Establish a community that is truly equitable for all races, genders and lifestyles. This includes women and all of the LGBT-connected communities,

including lesbian, gay, bisexual, transgender, transsexual, queer, questioning, intersex, asexual, ally and pansexual.

12. Give weekly talks to your employees to help them grow and be more effective. Include helpful hints in the area of personal development.

13. Bring in guest speakers to help your company expand its knowledge base.

14. If you believe co-workers to be in pain, or even if you're guessing, reach out to them. Buy them cups of tea and ask them about their lives.

15. Eat healthy foods and make sure they have only limited levels of sugar and caffeine.

16. Go for long walks with people you love. Hold hands.

17. Nurture the loving relationships in your life.

18. Dance in your living room as often as possible.

19. Instead of being on pedestals, be a little self-deprecating. Everybody loves humble leaders.

20. If things are heating up, slow down a little so that you can stay ahead of it all.

21. Establish mediation processes to help people work out their differences.

22. Admit that you're wrong when you're wrong.

23. Don't guess about someone's value, find ways to figure it out and put it to work within the company mission.

24. Follow thought-leaders and get to know their methodologies.

25. Open your heart to at least one mentor so that you always have a safe place to go.

26. Share your heart with your loved ones so that they can nurture you when things get tough.

27. Be generous when others need your help. If it's not you, do your best to help them find someone who can guide them along their path.

28. When you go to networking events, be yourself. Use your own personal language. Let go of the corporate lexicon. Be authentic, always.

29. Do really big favors once in a while. This feels great and it'll always come back to you.

30. If you can't ground it or dissolve it, step away from drama. It's not meant for you.

31. Call or hang out with close friends once a week.

32. When feeling stressed, take deep breaths. Be mindful of your moods and attitudes. Teach mindfulness and meditation to every employee.

33. When you're depressed, tell your closest friends. If they're not available, write in your journal. If you don't like to write, go for a long walk. Continue to seek ways to uplift yourself. Figure out what makes you and your heart happy and give yourself those gifts as often as possible.

The best managers are calm, firm, kind, forward-thinking, proactive and direct.

33 When Things Aren't Perfect

One thing I know: The startup world is both educational and entertaining. That being said, it truly sucks when your startup tanks. This usually means that you can no longer afford food, you're forced to sell your car, you're sleeping on some crack-head's couch, and the only lover you can score is in rehab.

You may have even considered killing yourself, but you can't do that. You're a beautiful, loving, inventive human being, and mistakes are part of life. Plus your story will inspire and educate others — but only if you're the one telling it.

Living is far more imperfect than perfect. There are actually no mistakes, there is only learning. It's just that learning is sometimes a muther-f*cker!

So what?! You spent a few years on learning things that won't make any sense until you're 60. Take a deep breath. Have patience with yourself. Apply the learning to your next adventure. Everything gets better with time. Well, except politics and leftovers.

Make sure that you write thank-you notes to all of the people who helped you, including the family members who are no longer speaking with you.

Reach out to your ex and offer to help with alimony for the kid she gave birth to after you bailed on her.

You'll also want to apologize for being a big fat jerk to your former founding partners.

Additionally, you might consider beefing up church attendance, learning how to meditate and getting a little better at being grateful. Just sayin'.

I know you might be feeling some pain right now, but consider the fact that in the US alone, investors fork over $1500 in capital every second, over $48B annually. Plus, over 100 million new businesses launch every year, with three businesses launching every single second.

Guess what this means?

There are infinite possibilities.

There's always tomorrow.

You'll bounce back.

This is just a pause.

Titrating off of the startup drug is damned near impossible. Just when you think that you've healed from the last venture, the one that claimed your left ovary and the brightest part of your soul, some product evangelist ropes you into another insane game of "Let's Change the World and Get Rick At The Same Time." It becomes a never-ending cycle of insane passion and self-denial.

The point is that you learned more in the first three months of your startup than you learned in the six years you spent at your four-year high school, and the seven years you spent earning that two-year associate's degree. It's all relative.

Get a hot meal, do your laundry, nurture the loving relationships in your life, then get back on the horse and ride that beast until you find a startup that shits diamonds. That's the goal.

Another goal might be to invent something that helps humanity by reducing pain and suffering in the world. If you could look into that, I'd really appreciate it.

Good luck and keep dreaming!

There is no wisdom but through emotion. Shine love and light on every shadow. Let it all out!

Always be seeking the light.

34 Things That Heal

You are a child of the divine, your life is a dream, and there is much more dreaming to do! Always remember that you are loved!

When our lives explode and our heads burst, or when we have blood streaming down our faces from wild, unpredictable rides and adventures, it's important to take a few deep breaths and pause before making any major decisions. It's time to heal.

When we nurture our minds, bodies, hearts and loving friendships, there's an outstanding chance (and a statistical probability) that we'll not only come back to life, but when we do we'll be 2x smarter, 3x more lovable and 10x more effective.

We'll also come up with better Big Ideas and create stronger, more defensible plans to bring them to life.

A big piece of our health depends on what we put into and onto our bodies. Reject soaps and toothpastes that have sodium laurel sulfates and other hurtful ingredients. Stop using deodorants in your armpits — that's one of the most sensitive areas of your body. Why clog it with chemicals? Be aware of the lies that companies tell you about their products.

Startup Confidential · Paul Wagner

Here is a list of healthy things that you can do to get your mind, heart and mojo back in gear. Some of these ideas are miraculous. May these things serve you as much as they've served me and my friends.

Meditation	Cleaning the House
Walking Among Trees	Giving Things Away
Steam Rooms	Foot Baths
Massage	Bach Flower Remedies
Dance	Therapy
Tantra	Art Therapy
Espresso	Coloring Books
Chocolate	Non-Sexual Cuddling
Mantras	Spiritual Masters
Prayer	Forgiveness
Silliness	Saying Goodbye
Adventures	Saying Hello!
Selflessly Serving Others	Letting Love In
Yoga	Wild Dances in a Field
Reading	Travel
Being Intimate with Others	Tea Ceremonies
Physical Exercise	Non-judgmental Churches

Seek out healing and nutritive products that are made without metals or chemicals.

Always be in pursuit of modalities that nurture your body, mind and heart.

Checklist #7

☐ Schedule regular hang-time with friends.

☐ Engage employees and acquaintances in conversations that do not involve work.

☐ Continue to evaluate potential pivots.

☐ Eat healthful breakfasts and lunches.

☐ Continually listen to and assess your CTO, CMO, COO and other key team members.

☐ Plan a special might for your sweetheart.

☐ Take three powerful business people to lunch.

☐ Perfect the company website so that it quickly educates and enrolls customers.

☐ Assess yourself and consider that CEO might not be the best role for you.

☐ Make sure that you are either paying yourself enough to live without stress, or that you have a part-time job to take the edge off.

☐ Research project management tools that can help your operations run more efficiently.

☐ Hold a special event and present your startup to an invited community. Serve Kombucha.

☐ Give generously in selfless service to others.

☐ Get out in nature and run wildly through a field. Shout, laugh and sing the entire time. Let it all out! Let the universe know that you're a wild beast!

35 YOU MADE IT!

You did it! You put in thousands of hours of sweat equity. You drank endless cups of espresso and consumed countless pints of local craft beers and shots of locally made whiskey. You hired people who you came to hate and fired people you loved. You went to over 350 networking events and had sex with interns in closets. You made 1000 mistakes and 20 super-hot decisions that lead you to an astounding level of success. Great job!

You've built an insanely talented team and you're in deep relationships with wealthy customers. You're staying out of your own way, letting feedback enlighten your path and you've earned the respect of investors. It's so fun at your company, it feels as though you're running a startup resort!

It's amazing when every box has been ticked and every department has momentum. It's also a little scary, right?

The biggest challenge is keeping your team tight, motivated and finely tuned. Now that they're feeling their oats, they might wander into traffic and get hit by a bus, or the competition! Stay on them!

Because your mission is still vulnerable, continue to keep a light hand in every aspect of the company. Always be ready to shine your personal ethos onto each department's methodologies. When you don't see alignment, give specific feedback, allow for everyone's input, then lovingly nudge your teams forward.

I was working with a woman who had a brilliant idea, a beautiful prototype and she was funded coming right out of the gate. She became so overwhelmed, that when she saw the funding in her bank account, she hid in her basement for a week. It takes time to adjust for success.

You're going to have so many incredibly motivated employees and partners throwing ideas at you, as if you have 20 arms to catch them all. Be careful not to get sucked into other people's passions because they could steer you and the company into left field. Stay the course you mapped out. It's been successful so far, why change it?

There's a huge weight lifted off of your shoulders, but it's only temporary. You've raised money and you're on your way to revenue, but you'll need to continue raising money for several years. I know, right? Remain mindful and grateful. Take one step at a time. Your path is well-lit and your vision is paying off! Way to go!

Adventures always have multiple levels. Prepare for each one. Stay humble and alert. Remember to enjoy the ride in every possible way.

GO GET 'EM!

YOU FINISHED! GREAT JOB!

As you grow your startup, remember to take good care of YOU and your loved ones.

(Including your heart, your mind, your hobbies, your fun and your relationships!)

Stay in the moment so that you can soak it all up.

ENJOY EVERY SECOND OF THIS EPIC JOURNEY!

Working with Paul

I love the world of startups and I love getting startups ready for investors. If you're looking for meaningful and life-changing help, read on. Otherwise, thanks for buying my book. I wish you great success!

Startups can be daunting. Some of the best money I've spent was hiring folks who knew how to take me through uncharted territory. There's nothing like having experts around to help to bring your dream to life.

Whether you're just starting out or finally ramping up, I can help you grow your team, vet your processes and build a sturdy foundation.

If you need technology development to build an MVP, my company **CreativeLab.TV** can help. We've created apps for hundreds of companies, from startups to Fortune 500 conglomerates. We'll save you thousands on your prototype and we'll you get to market.

You might need guidance to help you to be a more effective CEO. You might even need a part-time co-founder to fill in the gaps that challenge you most.

I help startups build better products, clean up messes, re-contract key players, fill out executive teams and create better, more achievable operating plans — all based on realistic thinking rather than fantasy.

In the process of helping startups to improve operations, product development, tech and more, I coach the founders and executives, helping them prepare for the exciting, uncertain roads ahead.

We'll dig deep into your goals and mission statements. I'll teach you how to think quickly on your feet and how to make empowering decisions in the heat of the moment. I'll help you to quicken your processes and determine which pivots will serve you best.

My approach isn't cookie-cutter. Working with me can be challenging. I won't pretend to support your ideas if I don't find them compelling. I will always cut to the chase and be straight with you.

Let's set up a time to talk about it. I'm looking forward to learning more.

— Paul

PaulWagner.com

CreativeLab.TV

Every time you learn something new, your life and business are enhanced.

Learn everything you can. The best CEOs continually advance their education.

Author's Favorite Books

Shambala, by Chögyam Trungpa

The Power of Now, by Eckhart Tolle

Leadership and Self-Deception, by The Arbinger Institute

A Return to Love, by Marianne Williamson

Work, Sex, Money, by Chögyam Trungpa

Venture Capital for Dummies, by Nicole Gravagna & Peter Adams

The Lean Startup, by Eric Ries

Peace in Every Step, by Thich That Hanh

Brad Feld's books: http://startuprev.com

Steve Jobs, by Walter Isaacson

The $100 Startup, by Chris Guillebeau

Be Here Now, by Baba Ram Dass & Hanuman Foundation

The Four Agreements, by Miguel Ruiz

Startup: A Silicon Valley Adventure, by Jerry Kaplan

The Rumi Collection, by Kabir Helminski

The Power of Intention, by Wayne Dyer

Competitive Strategy, by Michael Porter

Zero to One, by Peter Thiel, with Blake Masters

Business Model Generation, by Alexander Osterwalder and Yves Pigneur

Zen Mind, Beginner's Mind, by Shunryu Suzuki

The Personality Cards, by Paul Wagner

The Startup Owner's Manual, by Steve Blank & Bob Dorf

The Power of Broke, by Raymond John & Daniel Paisner

The Way of the Superior Man, by David Deida

Startup Nation, by Dan Senor and Saul Singer

The 7 Day Startup, by Dan Norris & Rob Walling

Creating Union, by Eva Pierrakos & Judith Saly

Originals, by Adam Grant

The Missing Piece, by Shel Silverstein

Lean Analytics by Alistair Croll and Benjamin Yoskovitz

The Multi-Orgasmic Man, by Douglas Arava & Mantak Chia

You Can Heal Your Life, by Louise L. Hay

The Field Guide to Human Personalities, by Paul Wagner

Elon Musk: Tesla, SpaceX, and the Quest for a Fantastic Future, by Ashlee Vance

The Course in Miracles by some awesome angels

The 7 Habits of Highly Effective People, by Stephen Covey

Awaken the Giant Within, by Tony Robins

The Innovator's Dilemma, by Clay Christensen

Patent It Yourself, by David Pressman & Thomas J. Tuytschaevers

Business Model Generation, by Alexander Osterwalder

Marketing Strategy, by Robert Palmatier and Shrihari Sridhar

Your focus on personal development will determine the degree to which you'll enjoy and benefit from the fruits of your efforts.

Links

- F6S.com
- Startuprev.com
- Investopedia.com/terms/l/llc.asp
- Blog.startupcompass.co/should-you-bank-on-twitter-yes-if-your-product-is-free-compass-benchmark-analysis-has-found
- Kauffman.org
- PaulWagner.com
- Paulgraham.com/really.html
- Statisticbrain.com/startup-failure-by-industry
- seriousstartups.com/2014/01/28/18-surprising-facts-entrepreneurship
- CreativeLab.TV
- Entrepreneur.com/encyclopedia/sole-proprietorship
- Whatis.techtarget.com/definition/corporate-culture
- Seriousstartups.com/2014/01/28/18-surprising-facts-entrepreneurship
- Onstartups.com/tabid/3339/bid/10561/12-Facts-About-Entrepreneurs-That-Will-Likely-Surprise-You.aspx
- Inc.com/peter-economy/23-surprising-facts-about-being-an-entrepreneur.html
- Interestingengineering.com/35-inventions-that-changed-the-world
- Inc.com/guides/2010/09/how-to-write-an-executive-summary.html

- Investinganswers.com/financial-dictionary
- Alexandercowan.com/business-model-canvas-templates
- Theinnovativemanager.com/the-innovators-canvas-a-step-by-step-guide-to-business-model-innovation
- Accountingtools.com/questions-and-answers/what-is-cost-structure.html
- Searchsalesforce.techtarget.com/definition/customer-segmentation
- Go.Forrester.com
- Hoovers.com
- InnovationWithin.com
- CreativeLab.TV
- Techrepublic.com/article/accelerators-vs-incubators-what-startups-need-to-know
- Forbes.com/sites/briansolomon/2016/03/11/the-best-startup-accelerators-of-2016/#7e978f5b47be
- Khaleejmag.com/business/best-startups-incubators-and-accelerator-in-the-world
- Entrepreneur.com/slideshow/290723#2
- CityAm.com

About Paul Wagner

Paul is a 5-Time, New England EMMY® Award winning writer/actor, corporate comedian and educator.

For over 30 years, he's toured the world as a speaker, writer, producer, consultant and showman.

Paul has written, produced, taught and performed for millions of people on TV, and for over 500 corporate clients in ten countries.

He is also the CEO of CreativeLab.TV. Clients include Aetna Insurance, Reebok, IBM, Google, AT&T and many startups around the world.

Paul has raised over $4MM for startup ventures, including helping to launch the global phenomenon, Will Ferrell's FunnyOrDie.com on iTunes.

Paul consults for startups around the world, and produces corporate events, custom corporate comedy shows, and group workshops and retreats.

Paul's poignant and funny lecture entitled, *Startup Confidential: The Raw Unfiltered Truth about Starting a Company* is both educational and hilarious.

To hire Paul to speak or engage his technology company, visit **PaulWagner.com** or **CreativeLab.TV**.

Paul's Books, Apps & Cards

Infused with 78 beautiful and inspiring personality images, **_The Field Guide to Human Personalities_** is a deeply engaging experience focused on helping human beings see and improve upon the personalities at play in their lives. (Soft cover, 244 pages, color, 8.5 x 11".)

Paul delves into the behavioral and spiritual aspects of each personality, providing gentle guidance and insight.

The Personality Cards include 78 colorful personality cards and an inspiring booklet. It's a mixture of Tarot and Jungian and Transpersonal Psychology.

Thousands of people use _The Personality Cards_ to source answers to questions about life, love and relationships.

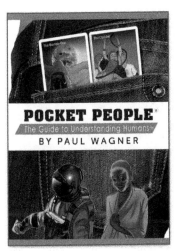

Pocket People: *The Guide To Understanding Humans* is full of helpful, on-the-go insight! (soft, 173 pgs, 4"x6")

Featuring 78 personalities, it's an easy-to-read exploration of personalities.

A great gift idea, this book will help you see yourself and others clearly. It's a fun and insightful read!

The Me App is an exciting mobile and web experience that provides helpful insights into you, your life and your relationships. It's FREE!

Select from a variety of unique personality readings or enter a few adjectives. The app returns sets of your temporary personalities. It's fun and eye-opening!

Use the app for personal exploration, or as a spiritual divination tool.

Share The Me App with friends and grow together!

Download now at PersonalityApp.com.

For inquiries:

Paul Wagner
paul@paulwagner.com

Paul Wagner writes, produces and publishes authentic works in the forms of books, plays, lectures, workshops, web & mobile apps, videos, movies and episodic television.

Visit **PaulWagner.com**